MY GIFT OF HERITAGE

My Gift of Heritage

YOUR PAST THAT WILL TAKE YOU INTO THE FUTURE.

Earl J Spivey Jr

Meadowlawn Ministries

Contents

Introduction

This is more than my story. Though it is centered on my family, it is really about all of us. I share experiences from a rural life in the 1960's. I openly acknowledge, and am appreciative for, the many who were, and continue to be, part of my life. I offer these stories first to my Children, Christine and Elliott. They are the inspiration for my writing. I hope to do more than just leave stories of their heritage people. I pray they, and you, will read what follows and be more aware and appreciative of our own heritage. We too often dismiss the past in our quest for the future. In doing so I believe we find only superficial and momentary achievements. The richer and deeper significance that makes living full and substantial grows from our being part of something much larger and bigger than our own individual life. I therefore invite my children to discover and live in the rich heritage I, and those before me, have left for them to continue. I invite those who are descendants of John Edward Prince and Isaac Jackson Spivey to discover some of their heritage and pathways worthy of walking. I invite all who *are reading to discover the value of your heritage and to choose to discover your family foundations. Then once done, live with a firm and honored life for those who follow you. Join me for life on a small southern farm. But more importantly, a reviving of heritage in each of our lives.*

One

A Little Boy Gets a Pony

For many boys it is only a dream. For me it was a dream come true. I was still in grammar school and just discovering what living on a farm was all about. The farm life had introduced me to animals and wanting a pony to ride seemed a natural progression. My father had begun farming

with mules when he was young. He had even run a dairy farm and delivered the milk by horse and buggy. He loved the animals and loved the farm life.

As a child I grew up with Kate and Luke the farm mules. By the time I developed a memory, Daddy was already farming with tractors. His first working tractor was an old John Deere M. However, he was still in the transition, as slowly as it came to rural South Carolina, from mules to tractors. When daddy bought the first serious working tractor Luke decided to flee the farm that same day. After having to chase him almost to town daddy took him to the sale and hence the glue factory. Kate was kept as daddy still preferred the mule for certain jobs that just seemed more natural and easy with a mule. Working the tobacco beds was one of them. I remember on several occasions going with my father to the tobacco beds, located at the back of the family farm about half a mile from the house, to prepare them for planting. He would go to the mule barn, just behind the house, and get Kate. He would put the harness and other gear on her and hook her up to a wooden flat sled. We would put the tools and materials needed on the sled and walk beside it or in front of the mule to lead her. More than once I remember hearing Daddy say, "Dod nemit that ol' mule." That was about as close to cursing as Daddy would get. What upset him was the sight of ol' Kate running as hard as she could all the way back to the barn. If Daddy still had much work to do we would make the half-mile walk back to the barn and lead Kate back to the beds again.

On a few occasions I remember Daddy looking over at me on the long walk back and saying, "Son ya' wanna' ride?" I of course said, "yes," and he would lift me up and let me sit on Kate's back until reaching the barn. I would hold to the harness and find myself in a whirlwind of fear and joy. Kate looked so big then and I felt so small on her back.

I only remember once being with Daddy when he used the mule to work the tobacco. I remember being on what my grandmother called the Scott Field. It was a high sandy hill and its topmost part was so sandy that the tobacco, which usually grew to at least shoulder height, never grew above knee height. That early summer was extra wet. The tobacco was getting high enough that it was time to "lay it by" as it was called. That was the time when the tobacco was tall enough that you could only make one last trip over it with the tractor. The John Deere M was extra high so you could wait a little longer with it. However, the time had run out and the weather was still so wet that the tractor would sink in the heavier dirt. By the time the dirt had dried enough to plow, the tobacco was too high to drive the tractor over it. So, Daddy decided to do it the "old fashioned way." He brought out the mule, dusted off the gear, and hooked up to the plow. I remember walking behind my father in the soft freshly turned furrow with my father looking the part of a farmer in the western movies following his mule and plow.

One of Daddy's well-preserved horse experiences came from his milk days. At the time most of the roads were dirt and horses and mules were still common. A family friend came visiting my grandparents riding in a horse and buggy. The buggy was nice and when the friend arrived, he tied the horse to a hitching post under some trees that provided shade for the horse. Sometime during the visit something scared the horse. The horse instinctively jumped backward trying to free himself from the hitching post. The reins gave way and the horse was free to flee. In the quick burst of energy and speed the buggy went bouncing off of three different trees and into many pieces. All they could do was to enjoy a roaring laugh and go retrieve the horse. The friend went home, but returned later that day to gather the many pieces of what used to be his nice buggy. Even today, when Dad and I talk about the event, he laughs thinking about that day so many years ago.

I, however, had only seen Roy Rogers, the Lone Ranger and other western heroes on our black and white TV and thought riding a pony would be great fun and a simple thing to master. So, I began asking Daddy if I could have a pony.

From time-to-time daddy would sell several cows from that year's crop for extra cash and additional help with our family budget. Every so often I would go with him. He would drive the cows up the wooden ramp that led them into the farm truck and then lock them in the truck bed. The truck bed was surrounded by wooden sides that were about six or seven feet tall. On one particular day we were going to Chadbourn, North Carolina, which was about forty-five minutes away. The market was basically for hogs and cows. Every once in a while, someone would bring some goats, ponies or other livestock to sell to anyone willing to buy them. This is the how the market worked: The farmer would bring his livestock and the owners of the market would auction the animals to the highest bidder. The animals would be paraded through a small area on which the auctioneer was on one side of the livestock and the potential buyers and anxious sellers sat on the other side. Most of the livestock was bought by packing company representatives or farmers wanting to bring new blood into their existing herds. The seating was arranged in a half-circle of wooden benches made like large steps.

We backed the truck up to the unloading area and the men sent the cows down a wooden hallway to one of many wooden fenced holding pens. After we parked the truck and returned to look at the different animals, we noticed a pen with several ponies. It was one of those moments when you could almost touch your dream. Almost, but not *quite. We talked about the ponies and Dad even talked with the man who had brought them.*

When it was time for the auction to begin, we took our places. We watched for our cows to come through and listened intently to try to understand the mumbo jumbo of the auctioneer so we would know what price our cows brought. I remember sitting by my father looking at the cattle and watching the men running the cattle into and out of the buying area. They would do some quick moving when an angry bull or uncooperative cow was chased into the area. The big wooden door swung open to our right and in trots a beautiful brown pony. His tail and mane were almost white and he just stood there unaware of what was really taking place. The auctioneer began and as he called out the price, someone to our left raised his hand and the auctioneer pointed to him and raised the price a little. And then I thought the auctioneer was pointing at me. I lost my breath and suddenly realized that Daddy was making a bid for the pony. I couldn't breathe, I just stared at the auctioneer and then my dad. I looked at another person lifting his hand and then the auctioneer and then my dad. He raised his hand once more and the auctioneer continued. And then... "Going once, going twice, sold to the man with his little boy." By now I had almost passed out from not breathing and suddenly I couldn't breathe for trying to take in what had just happened. I didn't know whether to jump and shout, hug my father or jump down to the holding area and hug the pony's neck. The dream I could almost touch was now in my hand. As we made the drive home, I kept turning around in the seat to be sure that beautiful pony was still in the truck.

When we arrived home, my four sisters, two older and two younger, saw the pony and joined me in what seemed to be Christmas out of season. We all couldn't stop rubbing the pony and talking to him while waiting to crawl on and ride.

I never rode like Roy Rogers. I actually fell off several times. We didn't have a saddle or bridle so those had to come later. To get them we turned to a familiar source, the Sears and Roebuck Catalog. Before long, this beautiful pony was wearing a new saddle and bridle and being treated like a king. My sisters and I named the new pony Lucky. We were all excited but scared as well. When we tried to ride him, he would walk sideways to the electric fence and rub against it giving us a jolt on our leg. After a while everyone became afraid to ride him and the little boy's dream came to an end at the same sale where it had come to life.

As I grew into High School, I wanted to get a horse. I talked it over with Daddy and we agreed to get one. Someone within just a few miles of our home had one they were no longer riding. They were willing to sell it to someone who would give it a good home. There was only one catch; the horse hated being put in a trailer. Nancy was gentle and a beautiful off-white color. She was healthy and had enough Arabian in her to prance around the barnyard with grace, pride and style. But riding her all the way home wasn't an option.

Daddy's trailer was a wooden homemade trailer for carrying cattle. It had sides that were planks of wood with six-inch gaps between them. It had a hinged door on the back left side and was about a foot off the ground. Sure enough, we could lead Nancy all around it and up to it but when her nose reached the door she planted her front feet firmly into the ground. Pull as hard as you want on the bridle but she wasn't going anywhere. Being a humane person Daddy wasn't interested in subduing the animal with brute force so we came upon another idea. I would lead Nancy to the door and get in the trailer getting her nose as close as possible. My father and my uncle who came with us would take a two by four, one on each end, and use it to lift her back legs up forcing her weight on her front feet. With a little shove forward, she was either going to go into the trailer or fall on her face at the trailer's door. They put the two by four

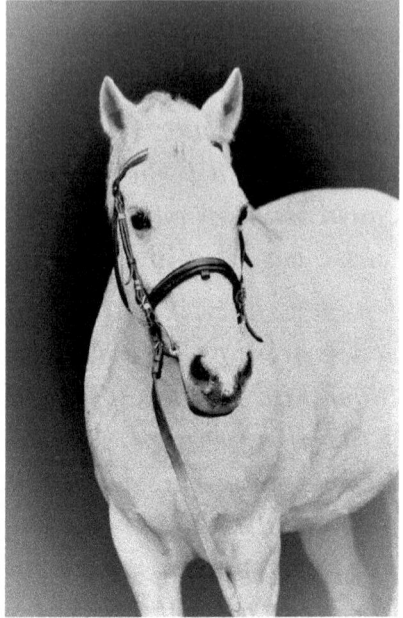

across her back thighs and gave a shove forward. Her front legs buckled and she lunged forward just enough to put her front feet on the trailer floor. With that she gently and easily walked into the trailer. That is how Nancy arrived on the Spivey farm. Unloading was never a problem, just getting her into the trailer.

Over the next several years I spent many Saturdays saddling up Nancy and riding over the Spivey farm. I often wished she was more receptive to traveling and that I could ride her somewhere other than the mile long border around the farm. The farm was bordered by wooded areas and fences that left riding confined to our own land. I remember on many occasions working the tobacco fields and seeing one of my cousins, who loved horses, come riding up on Nancy. I wanted to ride her and explore places other than the small farm perimeter but I had an experience a few years earlier that taught me not to ride her near the highway in front of my house.

About a quarter of a mile toward town lived a girl several years older than me. She loved horses and riding them. She had a Tennessee Walker Horse that was beautiful. It was dark brown and seemed as tall as the trees. On many days I would see her go by the house riding her horse. In front of my house was a railroad track and about forty-to-fifty feet further was highway 701. The highway was a major two-lane highway usually busy with cars, trucks and other vehicles for traveling and *hauling. She would ride her horse between the highway and the railroad that was mostly cleared and grassy for miles. Often we would hear our hunting dogs "rasin' cain," as we called it, in the back yard. We usually looked to see if my neighbor was riding her horse by which caused our dogs to lunge at the ends of their chains for an opportunity to chase such a large prey.*

On this particular day I heard the dogs barking and saw her riding southward between the railroad and the highway as usual. I thought no more about it until her father came quickly driving up to our house about an hour later. He told my father that the horse had become frightened by traffic on the highway and made a sudden jump that resulted in the breaking of its right front leg. It was every horse rider's nightmare. Repairing a broken leg on a horse was not only greatly expensive but was a long and uncomfortable experience for the horse. They, like many others, didn't have the money to pay veterinarians to house and care for the horse the long time required for healing. So the only thing to do was what so many have done before, shoot the horse.

Her father needed a flat trailer on which to carry the horse once shot. We quickly got a trailer he could use and I rode along with him to where the horse was. The girl was crying and greatly upset and the horse, usually tall and stately, could only limp on one front leg and look to us for comfort and help. The girl got into the car with her mother after a teary and painful good-bye to her long-loved horse. Once she left, we pulled the trailer beside the horse and her father did the unpleasant job of shooting the animal.

The situation was made worse by a fatal flaw in our planning. We had put the trailer on the side of the horse's good leg not realizing that once shot the horse would naturally fall to the side of the broken leg. So now the large animal was shot and lying on the ground beside the trailer. We were able to stabilize the trailer, as I had seen my father do numerous times to carry a shot cow to the Cold Storage for butchering, and pull the horse up on the trailer for transport. We now carried the horse to our family's animal graveyard. It was a sandy hill on the farm on which you could dig a fairly deep hole without getting into any hard dirt. An hour or two later we put the dirt back into the hole that had become transformed into another spot remembered for the resting place of a loved animal companion in life.

I therefore avoided riding along the highway and railroad tracks. I knew that Nancy was gentle but sometimes spirited and easily spooked. Another of my cousins would sometimes ride with me. He learned the hard way not to shake a limb when passing under it.

We had decided to go riding that morning. He lived across the highway in front of my house and we often played together and worked together on the farm. We saddled Nancy and I got in the saddle and he rode just behind the saddle. We rode to the back of the field and were headed back toward the house. We were riding along the edge of the field and passed under a low-lying limb of a sweet gum tree. I had learned earlier myself not to make unexpected noises while riding or I might find myself looking at Nancy running to the barn. As we came under the limb, I ducked to avoid it but my cousin decided to push it up with his hand and let it fall behind him. I heard the leaves on the limb rustle and grabbed for the saddle horn. I barely got my hand on the horn when Nancy shot out like lightening. My cousin went rolling off behind me and I finally got Nancy to stop and calm down about a quarter of a mile away. I went back to get my cousin but never had to worry about him shaking a tree limb while riding with me again.

Two

Snails, Shells and Puppy Dog Tails

Even the dairy had its dog.

It seems that even in many of the landscape paintings or various drawings of farm life there is usually a dog in the scene. It just seems natural, somehow, that a farm isn't complete without a yard dog. Growing up on a farm was complete for me. All my life I can remember at least one mutt, as we referred to them. My earliest remembrances were of a shorthaired dog of a light brown color. We called him Prince. Prince had so many additives to his pedigree that we never thought of him as of any particular breed, just a mutt. Prince loved to run with the tractor and follow us all over the farm. He would chase the rabbits and bay at the snakes. He was a friend to my sisters and me and a constant companion in our work and play.

Another of the special dogs was a longhaired cocker spaniel with black spots and speckles on a white background. We called her Snoopy, what else? My uncle lived uptown in our local town and we would visit with him, his wife and daughter from time to time. One day while visiting them and playing in the neighborhood we met Snoopy. We played with her and came to love this small and very friendly dog. We later learned that she had no home; just a community that kept her fed and let her play with their children. Since no one really wanted Snoopy we decided to give her a country home.

Snoopy took easily to the farm life. She loved the freedom of roaming and running without having to dodge and watch for traffic. However, she still had to learn how to avoid tractor tires. I remember once when using the old John Deere M in the

tobacco field. I was making a sharp turn at the
end of the row where a ditch was only a few feet
from the end of the rows. As I was turning Snoopy
wasn't quite quick enough on the ditch bank. The
front tractor tire ran across Snoopy's back legs.
Fortunately, the tractor was light enough not to
seriously damage her. She began to bark a bark of
fear and danced about on three legs with one of
her hind legs held outward. After a minute or two
she was able to lower the leg and in a few minutes
more, she was pretty much back to normal. She
did give the tractor tires a little more respect after
that.

Another time Snoopy found her long hair to be a
hazard. Snoopy, being a cocker spaniel, had long
hair on her tail and legs. That usually caused
little problems if any at all. However, farming
tobacco had its own hazards. Anyone who has
worked in tobacco knows of its nature. Tobacco is
really a weed but a highly cultivated weed. Its
large leaves and stalk are saturated with a tar
like substance. If you break suckers from the
stalk, crop the leaves or break the flowering tops
off the stalk, your hands become covered with a
black sticky substance that you can actually rub
off in little rolls and sticky balls.

We had cropped the tobacco several times leaving
about half the leaves on the top of the stalk. As
usual Snoopy was escorting us in our work and
her back and tail were constantly rubbing the

lower leaves and stalks. She was running in and out between the stalks that were planted about two feet apart. As Snoopy walked around one stalk, her always-wagging tail brushed against the stalk. Since she had been in the field and around the stalks most of the day her hair had by now become somewhat tacky. However, when the long hair on the tip of her tail hit the stalk, it stuck. With a yelp and intent of getting away from what was grabbing her from behind, she naturally tried to pull away. Her hair was stuck so tightly she did the next natural thing which was to turn and try to make it turn her loose. When whirling around she only rapped her tail around the stalk making matters worse. By the time we could get to her she had her tail completely rapped around the stalk and was yelping as if she knew she was about to die a long and painful death.

Lucky for us she trusted us enough to let us help her unwind without biting the hands that were trying to free her. We slowly unwound her tail easing her around the stalk until we could remove her longhaired tail from the sticky stalk. She must have learned her lesson because we never had to unwind her again.

There were many puppies and dogs that ran loose in our yard and on our farm during my childhood and adolescent years. Flip, Jack, BoBo, Clemson, Tiger, Prince, Rufus and Dufus were just some of them. My oldest sister was especially attached to Clemson, a part collie puppy and his brother

Tiger. Each of them can be remembered for some special quality or character that made them unique. For Snoopy it was her warm and loveable spirit. On many occasions I, and others in my family, would enjoy a warm few moments of human and animal affection by holding Snoopy in our lap and caressing her head and back. She was small enough to lie in our laps and affectionate enough to enjoy our attention. She was usually playful and always ready to follow us wherever we wanted to go.

There were few neighbors anywhere close to us other than my grandparents who lived on the farm with us. The farm had actually been my grandmother's given to her by her father and was willed to my father as a result of his working it for many years and promising to care for her and my grandfather until their death.

With only wooded land surrounding three sides of the farm and a highway on the other, the dogs were free to roam. However, they would sometimes wander onto neighboring property and not all neighbors shared our appreciation for animal companionship. Snoopy and some of daddy's beagles would sometimes run the woods around the farm chasing rabbits and occasionally a cat.

One summer afternoon several of the beagles were allowed to run and start building up stamina for the upcoming hunting season. They were gone for a short while when we saw them running back from a neighboring farm. We noticed that they were acting unusual. Before they reached us a couple of them collapsed and by the time Snoopy reached us she collapsed too. Within a minute or two they all lay dead. One of them had brought back some cut meat with him. It seemed that someone did not appreciate the dogs being on their property and had decided to eliminate the problem by poisoning the unwanted guest. It was a hard lesson in life. We all gathered on the familiar hill and buried the dogs saying our goodbye and knowing the warmth of Snoopy's presence would be greatly missed.

A part of farm life is learning to deal with death. As children we came to see the highway in front of our home as a stream of death. Many of our puppies that ran loose in our yard always made it to the highway and thus a messy spot on the pavement. We didn't go across the highway to work much except in the summer. During the tobacco season we would regularly go across the highway to take the tobacco for storing and later for final preparation before taking it to the warehouse for sale. As a result, the summer months were often marked by our dogs being determined to cross the road to go with us and thus discovering first hand the danger that usually led to death.

Rufus and Dufus were prime examples. Don't ask where we got those names but we did. It was even worse for my grandmother who could never remember Dufus' name. She gave up and just called him "Paduker." Rufus and Dufus were solid black puppies and loved running on the farm. We got them in the late spring and thus they were both quite young when we began our regular trips across the stream of death. I can still recall our screams and tears when the inevitable happened. We were working across the highway in the Milk Barn. It was called that because it was earlier used for the dairy Daddy ran. We had been trying to teach the puppies to stay in the yard and not go past the railroad tracks. As we were busy working, we looked up and saw the half-grown puppies crossing the railroad and coming to join us. There was little we could do. By the time we made it out the door they had made it to the highway and we could see it coming. The car tried to miss them but they were moving and that made them all the harder to avoid. We heard the thud and saw a lifeless form on the highway. One had been hit and the other narrowly escaped. It was Rufus. And my sister felt the bitter and painful dagger of death.

We took time to bury Rufus and took courage that Dufus was still with us. We were later to learn that "Paduker" was just too dumb to get run over. Dufus constantly amazed us with his unthoughtful antics. We enjoyed the many laughs he brought to us. He grew to be a sleek black and full-grown dog. He enjoyed the farm life for several years. He would run the fields and follow the tractor wherever it went. He was a constant bodyguard and amusement to us. He did learn to be rather smart about crossing the highway but had a weakness that eventually cost him his life.

During my junior and senior years of high school I only went for part of the day. I arranged to get study hall at the end of the day and was able to leave school by 1:00 or 1:30 every day. I would come home and get a late lunch and then go to the fields to help with the farm work. One day as I drove up in the yard, I saw Dufus lying in the grass. That was nothing unusual but he just didn't look right. I went over to see him and when he got up to greet me I could see what was wrong. He had a rambling streak in him and from time to time he would go visiting in the neighborhood or roaming through the woods. Across the highway was a bay, a large section of woodlands that grows thick, almost impassable, underbrush. Dufus had a habit of roaming the bay from time to time. When Dufus stood up I could see a steel trap attached to the paws of one of his front feet. He had that pitiful look of, "Can you help me?" And I could read his mind, "But if it hurts, I'm gonna' bite you!" I couldn't just leave him like that so I risked the bite to help him. I gently released the pressure on the jaws of the trap by pushing down on the two tension pieces that held the jaws tight. Fortunately, it was a trap designed for small game and didn't have sharp teeth. I held my breath and pushed down on the tension springs knowing any moment I was going to get an instinctive bite aimed at the producer of unwanted pain. Dufus only whimpered and as the jaws opened pulled his foot free. I think that cured him of roaming through the bay. I kept the steel trap in daddy's tool shed and thought of that day when I would catch a glimpse of it.

Dufus loved to be chased. He didn't find any particular joy in chasing cars. His great thrill came from the train. Dufus did what no other dog we had ever owned, or would own to this day, did. We never thought much about the train horn that sounded long before passing our house and long after passing as well. We just took it in stride. One day we were at the house when we heard the train's horn. We caught a glimpse of Dufus running toward the train tracks. We watched in *amazement at our dumb mutt. He ran to the railroad track and sat between the rails. He sat and sat and the train came closer and closer. He sat just watching it coming closer and closer to him and then, when it came to about fifty yards from him, he took off running. Not to the house but straight down the tracks in front of the train. He would run till the train would almost touch his tail and then make a leap off the tracks and watch the train go by. I watched him do it many times wondering which would be his last. One day it came. Daddy came and told me the news. Dufus had made his last dash. What actually happened we will never know but we can only imagine. Maybe he waited a second too late, or maybe his sure and trusted feet slipped, or maybe something distracted him. All we know is that he didn't make it off in time. His head and front legs made it but his trunk and back legs didn't. We took our dumb and loveable mutt to join the many others for his final resting place on the burial hill.*

I was in high school when my grandfather, who lived next door, died. He had been sick for a number of years and my grandmother had been his constant nurse. After his death someone thought a small dog would be a great companion to help ease the painful loneliness my grandfather's death left. So, one day they arrived with a tiny little puppy with thin blond hair. The truth is this dog was Uuuuugly. He wasn't so ugly he was cute. He was just uuuuugly. My grandmother decided to name him Trouble. I think she had some premonition about the future. If he wasn't so ugly, we could have been mean to him. But the poor soul looked so pitiful that you just had to be nice to him. We have often wondered if he was part rat. He barely had hair. He looked like he had the mange and was mostly skin and not hair.

If his lack of hair wasn't enough, he was also just a small thing not even big enough to ever think about challenging one of the many cats always around. He had little tuffs of hair on his ears and a long barely covered tail. He sought to live up to his name. Grandmother came to love this little bundle of ugliness. He was an ever-present company in the still and quiet house. He gave a sense of comfort whenever she returned to an empty house and a joy to see his excited welcome at her return.

Trouble was ever by her side through her final years. It kept her moving to take him outside for a walk, bathe him and care for him. Whether we grew to love this little ugly mutt or not, we had to be thankful for the company he gave my grandmother during her final years.

Three

Those Blessed Hound Dogs!

One of the many coon dogs.

My earliest recollections of hunting were dark nights with flashlight in hand following my father to where the dogs had a coon treed. Mom would help me get on lots of warm clothing. It seemed that coon hunting was always a winter thing. It was usually cold and the early darkness allowed more time for hunting before bedtime. Sometimes I made it home before falling asleep and sometimes the night's activities were just too much and once loaded in the old car, or later the blue farm truck, I'd fall asleep before returning home. It would all begin with a bunch of excited dogs being loaded into the dog box. Actually before daddy could afford a truck for the farm we would take the car. Daddy would open the trunk and load the excited dogs into it shutting the trunk lid until we reached the place for hunting. The trick was to get them in without one or more of them jumping out. The other trick was to shut the lid without getting one of their long and constantly moving tails caught in the lid. There were basically two indicators of that happening. One was a long hairy object protruding from the trunk. The other was the unmistakable yelping of a dog in trouble under the trunk lid.

Many nights as a young preschooler and grammar schooler I would excitedly get bundled up and put on my rubber knee boots and take to the dark mysterious world in search of the ring-tailed masked bandits. Seldom did we actually eat one of the creatures. I do remember a couple of times a coon hash that

was prepared and rather tasty. Mostly we would finish the trip that night, or if too late in the evening the next day, taking our catch to one of the African-American families living near us who always looked forward to the unexpected blessing.

At one time we used to skin the coons and sell their hides. We didn't get any big money for them but a few dollars a pelt added up and was some extra spending change.

Sometimes, though not often, we would arise early before daylight and go in search of the ring-tailed masked bandits. I was in grammar school when I invited a friend to spend the night with me and go hunting with my father and me the next morning. He came and early the next morning my father woke us and while we dressed, he loaded the dogs. We went just a mile or so from the house and down a dirt farm road. We turned the dogs loose and walked them across a cornfield that was already harvested, leaving only stubbles where the stalks once stood. It wasn't long before the dogs were barking, meaning they had run across a trail and were starting the chase. My friend and I listened for a few minutes and then, needing something more active to do, decided to have a corn-stubble battle. The land was rather sandy and this allowed us to pull up a cornstalk stubble and the roots would come up holding a considerable amount of dirt with them. By holding the stalk and turning your body around you could sling the stubble as a projectile toward your opponent. *Fortunately, our accuracy wasn't very good. However, we did amazingly score a hit or two and laughed as my father gracefully walked further away from us so he could hear the dogs.*

He was practicing a hunter's art that had to be cultivated and learned. It was the art of telling when the dogs are no longer chasing but have treed their victim. I say victim because you were never sure what was up the tree until your light found it and you could identify it. Most coon dogs aren't particular. If it leaves a scent on the ground, they will follow it and give chase if it runs. If it doesn't, they will bay it on the ground or against a log or tree hoping to capture and kill it as dogs just naturally do.

My father, when still in school, enjoyed taking one of his many childhood dogs skunk hunting. He would tell me of the experience of the dogs chasing a skunk, or pole cat as we often referred to them, and baying it against some object or running it down into its own burrow. He told me that a skunk couldn't stand its own smell. So if you close off his burrow entrance he will soon burst forth close by. He would take his rifle and kill the varmints that were bad for carrying diseases, killing chickens, pilfering eggs and other valuables from the farm. He also told me of many successful trips where he returned home and stripped off his clothing at the back door and went straight to the bathroom to scrub away as much of the smell as possible. His clothing was simply gathered up later and burned, or at other times buried in a hole. Sometimes like a trapped skunk they would mysteriously crawl out and lie on top of the ground. (I'm only kidding about that!)

We coon hunted until I reached junior high, then we mostly deer hunted. I can't say that I missed coon hunting all that much. I was never quite skilled at the many skills necessary for coon hunting. You had to learn to walk through thick bushes and woodlands in the dark of night with a small spot of light from your flashlight. While using the small area of light to help you avoid holes and stumps, logs and other objects that would trip you and send you falling to the ground, you had to avoid low hanging limbs, unseen spider webs and vines as well. I usually bounced from vine to stump hole to low hanging limbs grunting and struggling to stay up with the others.

Another very important skill that I still haven't mastered is walking a log. This is very important as you can imagine. The dogs don't seem to mind the creeks, ditches and standing water no matter what the temperatures. I, on the other hand, had no desire to get wet on a warm or cold night. It always seemed that at some point in the night there would be a wide ditch, that means any ditch too wide to jump across, which required this all-important skill. Many are the precious memories of getting half way across, and once in a while almost all the way across, before losing my balance and either jumping into the water to avoid falling, or just falling into it. The others would usually laugh and if we got back to a field near the vehicle to wait for the dogs to tree again would light a fire where I, and usually they too, enjoyed the warmth.

Another important skill is learning to walk through shallow water in knee boots without getting water into your boots. That takes skill. When the water gets up near the top of your boots you need skill at choosing where to step and how to gracefully move through the water preventing the water from seeping over your boots and soaking your toes. Being a young boy, my boots were not as high as my father's or the other adults usually accompanying us. As a result, I followed them and before I knew it the water was up to the top of my boots but several inches below theirs. And then I would step in a spot with a slight indentation and yep, my toes were wet.

One particularly cold night the dogs treed a coon across a shallow creek. We made our way to the creek and started across it. Halfway across it I found a hole and before I could get out both feet were wet. I knew my feet were cold but there wasn't much we could do but go on to the tree and then head home since it was already late. We finally got home about 1:00 am that night and when I took off my boots, I found that I could pick the ice off of my socks. Fortunately, I didn't have frostbite.

Another important skill is calling the dogs. That was usually reserved for the one who fed and owned the dogs because his voice was the one that mattered to them. The necessity of calling the dogs came from the fact that the last time they treed a coon and we were ready to go home we were usually a long way from the vehicle. Trying to put the pack on a leash, usually six or more, and lead them through water, underbrush and trees was dumb to say the least. Therefore, all along the way back you had to call the dogs and keep them close so we could all grab the dogs once back at the truck. Many nights were spent standing by the truck thinking of a warm bed at home calling dogs that were still ready for another chase.

On many occasions we had to leave one or more dogs that refused to return at our beckoning. One in particular was Spot. Spot was an interesting mixture of unknown pedigree. Whatever was in his ancestral heritage must have loved coon hunting. When we went to see Spot for the first time, he was already a seasoned hunter and full-grown. We arrived at a country home off a dirt road near a wooded area. We pulled into the yard with our dogs in the box ready for a night of hunting. The owner turned Spot loose and began telling us about him and why he was selling him. Spot was a good hunting dog but his weakness was that he didn't want to come home. The owner was simply tired of leaving him and having to return the next day to get him. Before he finished talking, we heard Spot barking just a little way from the house in the woods. The owner looked at us and simply said, "Looks like we'll be hunting here tonight." Spot was on the trail. Needless to say, Daddy gave him the money and Spot came to the farm.

He was a longhaired something or other. Whatever he was he loved hunting coons. Time and again we took Spot and the other dogs on a hunt and sure enough no matter how late it was, call all you want and Spot just kept on hunting another coon to run. We learned to just leave an old coat lying where the truck was parked and when we returned early the next morning there was Spot lying on the coat wagging his happy tail and ready for home.

Another dog Daddy purchased came from Kentucky. Somehow, he ran across a long-eared Black and Tan hound dog that could be ordered and shipped wherever desired. Daddy ordered him and was told when he would arrive. He was to be shipped by rail and would arrive at the only train depot near us which was about an hour away. We arrived late one afternoon at the train station. It was dark when Daddy arrived with the family all excited about seeing our new addition to the farm family. Out came a wooden crate and inside it was a long-eared Black and Tan with red eyes indicating he wasn't handling the train ride too well. We all got a good *look and into the trunk he went for one final ride to his new home.*

We were amazed at a dog that had ears long enough to lay in his food. If he wasn't careful, he would bite an ear by mistake. He stayed with us for several years and ran with the pack and added a deep long bark to the chorus of dogs in chase of the ever-quicker, in the sprint that is, coon.

Two of the coon dogs that stand out do so not for hunting purposes. Jip was a female that appeared to be part Black and Tan, of the short-eared variety. However, Jip was what we called an ill dog. She had only a limited loyalty and would bite anyone else who didn't respect her space. Daddy and I were the only two who could handle her, and I was usually scared most of the time. I remember once when daddy bought a new hat. He wore it to feed the dogs late one afternoon. When he came to Jip's chain she growled and snarled at him. He grabbed a stick and reminded her who the owner was but she always growled and snarled at anyone other than daddy or myself if they tried to grab her or get close to her while fastened or in the dog box.

Jip had a son named Sport. Like his mother he too was ill. However, Sport was a great hunting dog. He had a much admired and desirable trait. Sport was a silent trailer. That simply means that when he picked-up a trail and began to follow it he didn't bark like most dogs. Instead, he ran as hard as he could following the scent left on the ground. Then with no warning he would surprise his prey and scare the living daylights out of it. Not having any warning by the barking of approaching dogs the animal simply shot up the closest thing available. Once he treed his prey, he would bark a few times and hush until we would call out, "Speak boy, speak!" at which he would bark a few times more helping us identify the tree's location. We often went to Sport, and the other dogs, to find a coon up a tree that was not much larger than a bush and no higher than a basketball goal.

Sport had a built-in prey switch. If you took him hunting at night he hunted for coons. However, if you took him during the daylight, he hunted squirrels. Just like at night he never barked until the poor squirrel, suffering from heart failure, scampered up the closest thing available. I would take Sport on the farm to hunt squirrels and admired his work. However, once I shot the squirrel, Sport would grab him. Even though it was me reaching for the squirrel he would growl at me. I would usually wait for him to put it down and then I would pick it up and we would go in search of another.

Another skill needed for coon hunting is learning to hold the rifle up with one hand and with the other holding the flashlight behind your head so you could see the sights on the rifle barrel and aim it at the coon up in the tree limbs. Daddy was *amazing at this. I never figured it out so he was the solo gunman and displayed his skill and accuracy time after time. Once the coon is shot you have to stay clear of where it will fall. That is an important skill too. Once, a coon was way up in an oak tree which stood in a low-lying area with standing water all around it. The dogs were all excited around the tree trunk barking and jumping like they wanted to climb the tree and get that coon themselves. Daddy shot and suddenly right behind me fell the coon. Before I could move six dogs engulfed me in search of a taste of coon. Actually, they wouldn't eat it they just wanted the pleasure of thinking they had a part in killing it. By the time we could wrestle the coon from the pack of dogs I was wet from my waist down. That night I came home wet from the coon catching, not falling off a log.*

Four

'Backer Gethern'

At the bottom of the picture above is me, my mother and four sisters. Notice at the top, and in the background, the road leading to the barns and fields. The first barn on the right is the mule barn which was used for holding cows and for storing hay in the winter and tobacco during the harvesting season. The buildings just down the road from the mule barn are the two tobacco barns, a five-room barn nearest, and a four-room barn just past it. These have the large shelter built around them for storing equipment. The farthest barn is the oldest barn. It is a log barn, never used during my years.

Growing up in the country taught me a unique dialect of English. The skill was in shortening words, joining them together and saying them with a pronounced slur. As a minister and thus communicator, it has taken me many years to clean-up- my dialect. Even now I laugh at myself sometimes when by instinct I use one of my childhood phrases or words. An example is the following. English: Do you want to go with me to the tobacco sell tomorrow? Southern dialect: Ya' wanna' go w'id me to da' 'backer sale da'marah? English: What do you want to eat? Southern dialect: Wha-da-ya wanna eat? If you listen around Horry County, you still hear some of the old dialect and some of the words that continue among us today. Words like hope, which means "help." Someone may say, "Can I hope ya'?" Another is, "Just chunk 'da dishes in 'da zink."

If you hear someone refer to the outside water source or the water source at the kitchen or bathroom sink as a faucet you know that they are retrained or a foreigner to the Independent Republic of Horry, pronounced with a silent h, county. The old timers only refer to a spicket, (actually spelled spigot). You had a spicket in the bathroom, kitchen and various places outside. As you can see my spelling has been a lifelong problematic area for me. I spell the way I talk which was usually very different from the way the word is spelled in the dictionary. Even today I still enjoy getting around the old timers and listening to a dying and vanishing dialect from my childhood.

The tobacco beds, fields, barns and packhouse were places where the Southern dialect flourished. There was often the mixture of white and African-American people who learned to communicate with their own distinctive styles. And tobacco was a year around job that gave the ever-evolving dialect a continual opportunity to be taught, refined and developed.

During the early sixties the tobacco cycle started in the fall. The farmers would usually start the process by raking pine straw from some area that had pine trees. It might have been their own yard or someone else's. The forest was usually not a good place due to the limbs and other debris that lay on the forest floor. Therefore, the farmers could be seen raking a friend's yard around town to get the needed pine straw for later use. As fall turned into winter more serious preparations began. About Thanksgiving or Christmas, the farmer began preparing the beds. The tobacco beds were where the tiny seeds would be carefully nurtured into plants to be transplanted into rows in the field. The preparation of the beds began with selecting a proper site that had rich soil and

*was near an abundant water supply. Most would
select a site protected by woods on two or three
sides. Once selected the ground was turned with a
disc, if a tractor was used, or plows, if a mule
was used, to soften the soil. A good bed needed to
be soft, free from leaves, limbs and other debris. It
also needed to be as free as possible from the many
weeds that naturally grew in the fields.*

Gathering with mule and drag.

*In the mule days the
farmers would pile
leaves and other
burnable fuel on the
intended bed and burn
it in an effort to kill
weed seeds just below
the surface. By the
early sixties the
chemical revolution was in full swing and now the
farmers were aided by seed killing gasses. These
gasses came in small pressurized metal cans that
could be turned upside down and pressed down on
a sharp object, sometimes just a nail driven
through a board. The extra expense of plastic
holders was often rejected for the less expensive
board and nail.*

*When the beds were made ready for seed planting,
still a long way off, they were sized so a roll of
plastic would fit the width of them. The width was
usually about eight feet a standard size for the
heavy clear plastic used. By Christmas or the first*

of the New Year the farmer would carefully go over the beds one last time and treat it for the killing of weed seeds. Shallow trenches were cut along the sides and ends of the beds. Then the plastic was unrolled and spread over the bed. Next came the tricky part. Since the gasses were highly toxic the farmer had to either puncture the canister and quickly seal off the bed, by shoveling dirt on the plastic, or sealing it off first and push the canister down on the nail or holders especially designed just for that. Most farmers learned to use the boards and nails and still avoid breathing the toxic gas.

Once sealed and gassed the beds were left until late February. Some years later the farmers began paying a man that had a rig on his tractor that would run over the prepared bed and put the liquid chemical in the dirt, which turned into gas, and it also unrolled the plastic covering while distributing the liquid gas. As the contraption moved down the bed workers quickly shoveled dirt to seal the plastic down. In the long run it was cheaper than the cans and the additional work they caused. Once the tobacco bed was gassed and sealed the farmer had time to do other related jobs and even to enjoy some less demanding time. He may need to repair the barns that wouldn't be needed until mid summer, make more sticks to be used in the curing or find other odd jobs to help generate some finances to subsidize the farm work.

Had it not been for additional work my father would have had to abandon farming before I was born.

As already shared, my father ran a dairy during his high school years and for about eight years thereafter. The business was doing well and with my mother as his new bride he asked my grandfather, the financial backing for the dairy, to increase his salary. My grandfather felt that thirty dollars a month was plenty enough and made it clear that he would not agree to increase it. As a result, my father closed the doors of the barn and left in search of a new direction in life.

My mother, unlike my father, was raised in town. She loved the town life and I am sure was glad, even though the change was very painful, to move back to town. They moved to an apartment in the town where my mother grew up and Daddy went to work laying floor covering. Mom has told the story many times. She was enjoying the apartment and the town life. And then one night they were sitting in their cozy place enjoying a quiet evening together. They had been there several years and had firmly established their new way of life. Well almost. Daddy had some magazines like Field and Stream that he often thumbed through. Mom looked over at daddy and saw him just looking at one of his magazines. But something was different. He was just staring at a picture. It was the picture of a dog in an open field under a beautiful moon. At that moment she knew the apartment, town life and familiar surroundings of her childhood were soon to disappear. It was shortly thereafter that my grandfather and my grandmother, who was the actual owner of the farm, asked my father to return to the farm and care for them in their aging years and in return inherit the farm at their death. Much of what was on the farm was purchased by my father from my grandmother.

His first year back on the farm was a disaster. The weather remained dry and the crops simply dried up. He was able to borrow enough money to survive but needed extra income to subsidize the farm. He was asked to help at the post office as an assistant for a couple of the rural mail carriers. That job became a very important financial prop for the farm and later provided him with a retirement, due to his going fulltime years later. For most of my earlier life I remember Daddy carrying the mail on many Saturdays and at times during the week. It was often inconvenient and sometimes very frustrating, especially during the harvest season, but the additional money enabled him to continue farming. Similar stories are told by most all farmers. Few had the luxury of farming alone but had a part-time job that enabled them to continue doing what they loved most, working the land.

Once the coldest days of January and February passed it was then time for the actual planting. First you had to do what would be done time and time again, remove the dirt securing the plastic on one side and both ends. The plastic was then pulled back so the bed could be aired. The remaining gas needed to escape and leave the soil fertile and not toxic. This process had to be done several times prior to planting. The beds were usually covered at night for protection and uncovered the following morning. After the beds were sufficiently aired the hand tools came out.

The rake was essential. The beds had to be hand raked with a wide short-toothed rake. The process simply loosened the soil and removed any small objects left behind. Once the beds were raked soft and fluffy, they were ready for planting. The planting was simple. A small paper container, smaller in size than a snuff can, would hold plenty of seeds for planting five or more acres of tobacco. The seeds were very tiny and had to be mixed with something else for broadcasting over the bed. The farmer used this to his advantage by mixing the seeds in the fertilizer and therefore fertilizing and seeding the beds with one trip.

The fertilizer and seeds were mixed in a bucket and broadcast skillfully by hand over the bed. I can recall watching my father work like an artist reaching into the bucket getting just the right amount in his hand and gracefully throwing it over the prepared soil. It wasn't just thrown but thrown in a half circular motion that sent the fertilizer and seeds fanning outward and spreading the seeds in a uniform manner. If you weren't careful the seeds would be thrown in streaks and the plants would later come up in clusters rather than evenly over the beds.

Later the hand turned spreader made the job a little easier. We always had one hanging around the barn. It was a canvas bag, which opened to about the size of a large bucket, with a strap used to hang it around your neck. At the bottom of the bag was attached a wooden contraption with a rotating handle which turned a revolving circular plate under the bag. The centrifugal motion would send the seeds slinging out in front of you evenly covering the prepared beds. I first remember Daddy mixing the seeds and then spreading them by hand from a small galvanized bucket. Then he started using the spreader. Year after year the mixture was poured into the canvas bag, hung over his neck, and then the familiar march up and down the middle of the beds to spread the seeds evenly on the beds. Once the seeds and initial fertilizer was spread a final light raking was applied to help settle the seeds in the soil. The plastic was pulled back over the beds and again it had to be secured down by shovels of dirt, a never-ending job.

What had just taken place was the crude construction of a greenhouse. The farmers knew that to have plants large enough to transplant into the fields shortly after the last frost he had to plant the seeds long before that frost. Tobacco being a tender and sensitive weed, would easily die if left uncovered in even a light frost. To solve this problem a miniature greenhouse was constructed. The heavy plastic would trap the warmth coming from the soil and prevent even a light freeze from killing the tender sprouts and tiny plants. At first the pine straw was used to raise the plastic just off of the ground so the tiny sprouts would not be harmed. As they grew rows of wire were used about six inches off the dirt. Later the rows of wire were replaced with pieces of wire about two feet long that were cut and stuck in the beds making an arch that held the plastic above the plants. Leaving the plastic on the tiny plants on a warm sunny day would turn the miniature greenhouse into an oven and kill the plants too. So the poor farmer was left to uncover the beds most every day and return before dark to cover them in case of a light frost. The coming of meteorological advances greatly helped the farmer decide whether to cover the plants each night or leave them out under the stars. Without them the farmer was left to use his careful skill in weather predictions or simply cover them to be on the safe side.

As February turned to March the fieldwork now began. The two main crops for which the fields were prepared were tobacco and corn. Corn was for feeding the animals and the family. Many foods were made from corn, the most familiar being grits and cornmeal. Corn was a food staple for the livestock, especially the working livestock. Tobacco, on the other hand, was a cash and pleasure crop. Cash because its purpose was for selling and providing much needed finances. It was a pleasure crop in that some was kept for smoking and chewing. As children we would sneak out to the barn and crunch up a crispy leaf and put it in a moist, and soft, leaf to roll-up for smoking. If we got caught our butts would be smoking too. Both of these crops are called "row crops." That simply means they are planted in rows and worked throughout the summer. Corn was hard work but nowhere near the work of tobacco.

By the time early spring arrived it was time to break the land and start preparing it for the rows that would later be planted in either corn or tobacco.

Our John Deere 40. A single row tractor.

Whether you were working a mule or a tractor, the warming trend of early spring meant fieldwork. The implements were basically the same. The motorized revolution just enabled the farmer to do more at one time and to work much faster than with the mule. That meant that he could work a greater amount of the crop in the same time worked before. The expenses were greater but the returns were multiplied as well. That has been the *death spiral for so many farmers. With the transition from animals to powered equipment came another transition. This one took place in the home. It was the transition from the simplistic living to the comfortable living. With the spread of electricity, fossil fuels, and the manufacturing revolution into the rural areas came the thirst for purchasable things designed to make living more comfortable. Electricity gave people the potential for the many electrical driven appliances that today are viewed as necessities. Everything from hot water heaters, clothes washers, water pumps, lights, toasters and electric and gas stoves opened Pandora's box of human desires for a more comfortable life. As always there was a cost that had to be paid in cash. Thus the new debt system of payments, monthly or annually, opened the door for greater possibilities that the rural folks never before considered. The thirst for comforts fueled the need for cash flow.*

Out on the farm a much similar transition was taking place. As the farmer felt the need to expand his crops in order to provide more revenues, the way to do this required increasing debt. The banks were willing to lend the farmers money, at a small interest, and the stores were willing to sell for annual payments. In return the farmer now had a greater financial burden that demanded greater effort and risk to increase production and provide larger profits. A bad year after a new equipment purchase, or comfort items for the home, and the farmer was literally behind the eight ball. As a result, many small farmers were disappearing even in the 50's and 60's. Those on the edge found themselves finding part-time work and seasonal work that still allowed them to work the crops and the farm. Even without the new items of comfort the growing demands of producing more profit to deal with the increasing cash cost of living was choking the farmer. Such was the case of my father.

My grandmother inherited the land from the highway to the west side of the farm. The land across the highway, on which the dairy was built, belonged to her brother originally. During the time of financial stress and poor weather conditions, her brother lost the land his father had given to him to the banker. My grandfather went to the courthouse when the land was to be auctioned off for the taxes and debt and purchased the land for the owed debt. When my father returned to the farm in the early fifties he was starting on a financial shoestring. As previously mentioned, the first year was a big failure. Through much hard work and great self-denial, he managed to keep the farming dream alive and make it through a second year that brought profit and much needed relief.

We lived in a simple constructed and very plain house. My father did all the work except the building of the fireplace and chimney, the wiring and plumbing. At the time the plumbing consisted of a kitchen sink and hot water heater. The *bathroom wasn't plumed and completed until years later. We heated with a wood heater until I was in junior high school. Daddy borrowed $2,500.00 to complete the house after moving back to the farm. All his farming life he walked a tight wire where he had to balance financial limitations and a desire for comfortable living. In order to stay on the farm, we simply had to adjust our style of living. Dad has always been content with very little. Perhaps it came from growing up on that same farm and never seeing much else as a real possibility. Or maybe it was just a love for the farm that made all the sacrifices worth it. Mom had grown up a girl of the town and enjoyed the town life. Her father was a respected businessman and sought to provide his family with the simple comforts of the day. Life on the farm for her has always been trying and a life that necessitated a deeper strength on which to rely.*

Faith taught her to look for fulfillment not in self-indulgences but in the experience of living life with dignity and spiritual integrity. That integrity made the reality of God's oversight and shepherding a part of each aspect of our living, whether in the field or in the home. A determination to be people living by the Bible steered us away from the luring traps that so many fell into in the name of comfort and want. It gave us a deeper insight into the real essence of life. It also enabled us to look way beyond our own discomforts and see a much greater intent for life and the genuine inner peace that comes in surrendering to it. That was her secret for living without. That became the divine strength that protected her from demanding some of the simplest comforts that would bring financial stress and a comfort without real personal fulfillment in life.

Many farmers just grew tired of doing without. Many had families that refused to live the most simple and basic life style. Many wanted for themselves. And many just found that farming could no longer pay its own way. As a result, many farmers became laborers in other vocations. The old landowners were left to rent their land to the few farmers who were able to make a little money by farming greater quantities. When I was born, a family could get by on a few acres of tobacco and some corn. By the time I finished high school any farmer still farming was looking for thirty to forty acres of tobacco and feeling the spiral dragging him downward. Worn out and out-dated equipment had to be repaired or replaced. Either you went in debt and worked a little more next year or you kissed your dreams goodbye and left farming. Many suffered and held on to their dreams, and love, too long and felt the bitter agony of bankruptcy. Others felt the bitter dagger of dashed and unrealized dreams and moved off the farm and contented themselves with the greater comforts of a more lucrative occupation. Some never severed their ties with the land and lived a split personality between public work and farming around their work schedules. Only a very few were able to live the life so much loved as a farmer. But even they discovered the farm life was a bygone. The growing demands and necessities of farming such large acreage had turned farming into another business institution. For many the demands kept them off the tractor, out of the barns, and almost off the farm. Their time was devoted to dealing with employees, financial paperwork and business-type matters, the ever resolving of troubles and the constant worry of greater debts and shrinking profits.

Dad was blessed to make the transition late in life. He saw it coming and was able to get most of us through school before breaking the tie with farming. After I left college and no longer returned home each summer to farm, Daddy took a fulltime position with the local postal service and began working on a retirement that all his years of farming had neglected. He was able to keep the farm working some cows and small acreage, pleasure farming you could call it. The tobacco was cash rented and most of the land was rented along with the tobacco. Unlike many other farmers he was able to retire with something other than Social Security to sustain him and help pay the growing taxes on the land.

With the blowing of the March winds came the familiar sounds, smells and aches of farming. By the time I was old enough to remember much about the farm life, the tractor was in full use. The bottom plows were connected to the tractor and the land was turned upside down for about ten inches. This put whatever was growing on the top on the underneath side and broke up the hard soil. Next came the disc, which basically flipped and tossed the top six inches of soil to make it soft and workable. Then came the cultivating frame with plows and hillerblades, we called them, to form rows that rose about a foot. The hillerblades were round metal disks, much like a plate from the table, that were attached to the lower end of a round metal shaft that extended downward toward the soil. As the tractor moved forward the metal disk, about sixteen inches across, would spin. The hillerblades were turned at an angle so the movement of the tractor would cause the disk to cut into the soil and throw it to the center. With two hillerblades opposite each other you could roll a significant amount of dirt into a row. The plows followed the blades and formed the furrows that would be worked time and again.

How do you go into an open field and layoff nice long STRAIGHT rows? Farmers had a trick. It was simple as most tricks are. You take your attention off of where you are and focus on where you are going. The first row was most essential because once it was run you would thereafter have a furrow to follow with one of the tractor's wheels. A pastor from my childhood days relayed the story of one of his earlier experiences. His father sent *him out to layoff the rows for planting. He gave the advice to pick an object at the other end and keep your eye on it as you moved across the field. He did so but was confused when at the other side of the field he looked back to see a crooked row. He looked to his father with a questioning face. His father spoke sternly, "Son you are supposed to pick out a stationary object, not a cow!" Most farmers had two sticks that stood about ten feet tall. On the end of them were white material making it easier to see from a distance. When the first rows were being run a stick would be staked at the end as a target for making the row straight. I thought that was a rather simple task. I excelled at turning straight rows into crooked rows, a more difficult task. Daddy would sometimes get upset at my crooked corn and bean rows. I would remind him that I learned in school that you could plant more seed in a crooked row than a straight one. He was unimpressed and simply said, "Keep 'um straight Earl J!"*

The normal setting of the rows was about four feet. The tractor tires were set for that distance and until I reached Junior High, we only worked one row at a time. For the farmer time wasn't a major concern until the pressure of doing more in less time began creeping in. Work was just what you do on the farm. No one expected to get more done in less time. Everyone just expected to work till the job was finished and then move on to the next. Farming was one long continuous cycle that took all year to complete.

After the rows were made, by late March or early April, the rows were prepared for planting. Since the soil was used year after year fertilizer was essential for making a crop. The fertilizer was purchased in 100-pound bags. There was a particular type for tobacco and another for corn. Thank the Lord that when I came along it was only 100-pound bags. Daddy told me of his early days when fertilizer came in 200-pound bags. He said that he could tote, or carry, a 200-pound bag from the wagon to where the mule and distributor was. I have had many other men tell me similar stories from their years on the farm as well. By early junior high I had received the honor of filling the fertilizer distributor each time Daddy would complete one round. He would go down one row and back up the other. Doing so would use most of the fertilizer in the reservoir. He would then back the tractor to the trailer or truck bed, whichever was being used, and I would be ready with an open bag to fill the reservoir as full as possible and send him around again. The good part was being able to move the truck occasionally and not having to work continuously. As long as the truck was in its proper place and the fertilizer was waiting Daddy, who always drove the tractor, was happy.

Once the rows were laid off came the never ending running of them with differing equipment. Next came the distributing of the fertilizer and then plows to soften the soil and shape the rows. The plants were planted and then it was time to run them again to keep the soil soft for the expanding roots. Then you would run them again to kill small grass and weeds. And then if Daddy didn't have something else for you to do you could always run the rows. It wasn't until the corn or tobacco was too tall to pass under the tractor without damaging it that the row running stopped. In tobacco farming the fifth row was not planted so you would have a place to drive the mule and drag or tractor and drag during harvesting. The fifth middle needed from time to time to be run to keep the grass and weeds down. It was also used for spraying the tobacco, an essential for killing the little suckers, small sprouts of new growth from the stalk, and many worms and tobacco eating insects.

Between the caring for the tobacco beds and the running of the rows March turned into April and it was time to transplant the tobacco plants to the rows in the field. This usually didn't take place till after Easter. The tobacco plant was very sensitive to cold and one light frost would kill the plants in the field. It would kill the plants on the beds as already mentioned. To grow the plants and keep them safe until after the threat of frost a two-step method was used. First was the plastic as mentioned earlier. However, as the plants began to push against the plastic and the weather grew increasingly warmer during the day the plastic was replaced with a canvas mesh. It looked much like heavy cheesecloth. All during my childhood I can remember seeing the material hanging under the barn. If care was taken it could be used several years and the cost for using it reduced. By the time I reached Junior High the cloth was no longer used. The farmers began tearing large holes in the plastic for venting and avoiding the cost and added work of using the canvas.

As April came the plants were now about three inches in height and thick as carpet on the beds. Getting these plants ready took many times of watering them and from time to time adding nitrogen to quicken their development. Once about six inches or so they could be pulled by hand and rapped in burlap or placed in boxes. The wax coated chicken boxes from a grocery store worked well. The coating made the boxes durable in the wet work. It was wet because to pull the individual plants without loosing their tender root system the beds had to first be soaked with water. Then once wet the pulling started.

Pulling was backbreaking work. As mentioned earlier the beds were about eight feet wide. That meant that to pick the bed you had to get on the beds. After the first pulling you had to be careful to use the same footprints to avoid killing plants unnecessarily, or being injured unnecessarily. To *pull the plants required you to simply bend over and constantly work between your ankles. It is about like standing flat footed and washing the floor all day. Needless to say, your back didn't take long to complain. The good side was that once the larger plants were pulled it would take several days for the plants left to grow big enough to pull. On our small farm I remember many days that my father would pull plants all morning and part of the afternoon. Then when my sisters and I came home from school we would get on the setter, which was pulled behind the tractor, and set-out the plants daddy pulled, till dark. This slower process continued for several weeks due to the beds being systematically pulled at a much slower pace.*

Once the plants were in the field the work continued. If cutworms or budworms were a problem, we all got a special homemade device to combat it. Daddy knew that to get the budworms in particular poison had to get into the bud that closed in late afternoon. The solution was simple. Wooden sticks were attached to metal oil cans. Yes, oil used to come in one quart metal cans. The cans were attached to the bottom of the stick and the top cut out and holes punched into the bottom. The granular or powered poison would then be put into the cans and we would walk the rows and shake the can over the buds dispensing the poison into the buds. Year after year we would walk row after row shaking the poison in each bud or on each plant to kill the cutworm. It wasn't until later years that poisons were available to spray and kill the worms. April turns into May and on toward June. The danger of budworms and cutworms passes but weeds become a battle. The rich soil and preparations for the tobacco weed also promotes growth of unwanted weeds. If they grow in the furrow the plow will do the job. Even if they grow on the sides of the beds the plows can reach them. But if they grow on top of the row between the tobacco plants the hoe gets them. That means that somebody has to make the hoe work. Daddy always had an ample supply of hoes. Day after day we would get what the tractor and plows could not. Also, once the tobacco was laid-by, the last trip over it with the tractor, any weeds had to be removed by hand.

By mid-June it is time to walk the rows again. Now the problem is suckers. Suckers are the little growth buds that come up where the leaf grows from the stalk. They drain precious energy and resources from the leaves, which is the whole purpose for growing tobacco. So, when the spraying didn't get all the tender new buds, we had to remove them by hand. And, that was every summer. It always seemed that we came home for summer vacation just in time to go to the field and break-off the suckers. Suckering, as it was called was a never-ending job. Even when cropping began the off days were spent suckering.

Then there was topping too. Topping was the process of removing the flowering tops from the stalks. The tops were the reproductive seedpods of the stalk. The good news is that once removed they do not grow back. The bad news is that once they are removed the suckers grow to replace them. If not removed the suckers will produce the flowers and seedpods as well.

It seemed that just about the time topping began in early July the heat was at full force. The heat was made worse by the height of the stalks and leaves that filled the rows. The stalks were usually about six to seven feet tall. Even tall people found the work hot and stifling. But it had to be done and it would be many more years before a machine was created to remove them. Topping was a slow process. It was also a painful task. If the tops were tender, you could easily grab them and pop them off with a quick motion of the wrist. If they were more mature, already developing the woody fibers inside, it required more effort to break them off. This led to sore and tender hands as the lower part of the hand became sensitive in the constant strain. Daddy had a special box to help with this. It was a collection of broken pocketknives. When we complained of sore hands, he would pull out that cigar box of knives and give us one to use. We would tape our thumb and index finger to prevent cuts and soreness from using the knife to cut rather than break the tops. From one end of the row to the other we would slowly go from stalk to stalk, sweating and baking in the heat, until we reached the other end.

One of the enjoyable pleasures of the constant work was refreshment time. Whether we were suckering, topping or putting-in, cropping the leaves and putting the tobacco into the barn for curing, each day had two sweet anticipations. In the morning about ten o'clock and in the afternoon about three o'clock mom would make a run to the local store and return with Pepsi and crackers. We would drink our Pepsi's and eat our crackers, honey buns, cinnamon buns or sometimes peanuts, and talk as we took a much-anticipated break from the demanding work.

The heart of the tobacco season was gathering or putting-in. The words were used interchangeably. The process involved removing the tobacco leaves that were ripened from the stalk and putting them in the barn for the seven-day process of curing it. It usually began about July and continued through August and even sometimes into September. It was the most intense and pressure filled time for the farmer. The whole year's crop hung in the balance of what now was taking place. It is that time of year when the farmers act like they are going through menopause. Everybody knew that during July and August you just got out the way and left the farmers alone. They only had one concern on their minds, getting the crop safely into the barn and packhouse to prepare it for market so as to receive the highest price possible. This was the make-it or break-it months *and everyone in the farming communities knew it well.*

It all started with the cleaning of the barns. Various items discarded and placed under the barn shelter over the year now had to be removed and room made for bringing in the tobacco. In the early sixties when my memory bank began to build the tobacco was strung by hand and hung on sticks that were hung in the barn for curing. There were four croppers in the field. The drag-boy, usually a young boy who drove the tractor with the drag that was used to carry the cropped leaves to the barn for stringing, would pull down the fifth row. Tobacco was planted in four rows then a blank row, the fifth row, four more rows and another blank row and so on across the field. The drag would be pulled down the blank or empty row and two croppers would crop the two rows on each side covering four rows at a time. They would crop about three leaves per stalk and sling the leaves under their other arm until they had a large armful of leaves. Then they would go to the drag and place the leaves orderly on the drag. When the drag was full it would be pulled to the barn while another drag was being filled. Once in a while the croppers would get ahead of the barn help and get a well-deserved rest. But usually, the two parts would just work in a constant speed that continued until the barn was full.

When the drag reached the barn six people were waiting. The drag would be pulled under the shelter, right at the barn's door and disconnected. An empty drag would then be connected to the tractor and taken to the field to be refilled. Three people stood on each side of the drag loaded with tobacco. Two would hand the third person small handfuls of about three to four leaves. The third person who stood in the middle would toss a ball of tobacco twine down her tucked in shirt keeping hold of the end of the twine. The end would be tied to the stick and the handfulls of tobacco would be gently looped and tightened on the stick. The ball of twine was tossed into the stringer's shirt as a place for the ball to be unwound and yet contained. The barn help were usually the women and small children. I remember as a young boy having the responsibility of picking up all the fallen leaves and keeping a supply of sticks for the stringers. The sticks were about one inch square and five feet long. It was an art in motion to see the women with grace and speed taking hands of tobacco from the right and then the left and holding them close to the stick while looping them with the other hand and tightening them to the stick without cutting off the stems with the string. I tried a few times myself and admired all the more the gentle speed of the well-trained stringers.

Also at the barn was the hanging crew. The hanging crew consisted of two or three persons. One person carried the sticks of sewn tobacco into the barn and handed it up to the person or persons hanging them. Let me help picture the barn for you. You may have seen them in the fields of the south. A barn was usually sixteen feet square. It would have two wooden doors on two opposite sides. Often there was a tin shelter all the way around the barn. This was used for working in the shade and also as a place to store farm equipment. The inside of the barn was divided into four sections four feet across and the full length down the barn. The three dividers were two by four pieces of lumber that hung the sixteen feet and started about five feet off of the ground and ran to the ceiling two feet apart. If you walked into the door, you would see four rooms divided by two by fours, called tier poles, which allowed you to hang sticks of tobacco on them the entire length of the barn. Thus, barns were often referred to as four or five room barns. Once in a while you would hear of a six room barn. The hanging crew was responsible to hang the strung tobacco in these rooms in such a fashion as to put the maximum amount in it but not so as to prevent the flow of air that would leave the stems green and undried or the leaves damaged by the lack of airflow. This required a different spacing for the bottom leaves on the stalk and the top leaves.

Making the process more difficult was the many burners with covers that were scattered inside the barn to heat the barn. Most common was burner covers that resembled wire baskets turned upside down. There were usually nine in a four-room barn. Moving about required a certain grace and presence of the mind. Many have been the groans of those who moved to avoid a burner and forgot the tier pole only five feet off the ground. My head has many reminders that wood is harder than the head no matter what my parents said to the contrary.

The croppers gathered the leaves in the field, almost exclusively men, and the women and children strung it at the barn while the men hung it in the barn. At the end of the day the barn would be filled and the doors shut and the burners lit. Tomorrow we all reassembled at the break of day to do it all over again. Once the barn was filled and cured for the first time in the season you had to take-out the barn before filling it. That required getting up an hour or so earlier and removing the cured tobacco and placing it in neat piles in the packhouse and then going to the field to refill the barn.

The tobacco curing process had essentially three stages. The first was a process of wilting and turning the leaves from green to yellow. As the heat was set just above 100 degrees the leaves would naturally wilt and at the same time begin turning a bright yellow. This worked best on the upper leaves that had more body. The lower leaves, sand lugs they were called, were paper-thin and usually came out brownish. The real money was in the upper half of the stalk. It was these leaves that gave the cigarettes their flavor. The farmer was trying to cure the tobacco in such a way as to keep it visibly appealing and of a good quality texture. Not adjusting the heat properly could ruin both of these desired results and the higher price they brought.

As the wilting occurs and the leaves begin turning yellow the heat is raised. The thermometer is pushed up to about 140 degrees and the "setting the color" is started. The barns were most often about twenty feet tall. That meant that the process took longer for the upper tiers of hung tobacco to do what is done on the lower tier poles. Daddy was always the person who cured the tobacco and knew how to look up into the barn in the stifling heat with a flashlight and tell when it was time to set the color. The wilting and coloring would take about two days and the setting of the color would take an additional day to day and one half. By the end of the setting of the color stage the temperature was up to about 150 degrees.

By the time I arrived in the mid fifties the transformation from wood heat to gas or oil heat had already taken place. Daddy's young years of curing tobacco required a long winter of cutting and splitting wood. It also demanded someone to stay at the barn all night and be sure the heat is maintained with just the right amount of wood burning. That was a difficult experience of working around a warm fire in the wee hours of the night and forcing yourself to stay awake. The transformation to gas and oil burners provided several big benefits. First, the heat could be

*controlled by thermometers that would
automatically keep it at your preference. Second it
was a much safer way to keep the barn heated.
Barn fires were common and even with the new
burners the falling leaves would sometime catch
fire and soon the entire barn would be in flames
and the family in tears. It was said that my
grandfather, who worked in Virginia catching
moonshiners, brought the first tobacco curers into
Horry County. There is no documentation of this
and whoever was first wasn't the only one for long.
The farmers were looking for better ways to
harvest the crop and increase the profit for their
family's good. For many years I worked in the
barn we believed to hold the first gas curers in the
county. They were about five feet long and were
made of galvanized metal. The sheet metal came
up both ends and secured a top, much like a house
top shape, to protect the burner from falling
leaves. The long pipe burners were of two sizes
and were protected on the sides by eight-inch
strips of the galvanized metal running the length
of the burner unit. Six of these burners sat in the
barn and were connected to a large LP gas tank
behind the barn. The little burners were used to
wilt and color the tobacco and then the larger
burners were lit to push the heat up for setting the
color and drying out the stem. The other barns
had burners much the same as those used in
outdoor cookers today. They stood upright and
were circular in design. A large wire basket with*

a sheet metal covering for the burner was placed over each burner.

A third benefit was the more evenly spreading of the heat. The more evenly the heat was spread the more uniformed the curing process could be done. Many of the farmers went with oil instead of gas. Some of them regretted not using LP gas when their oil burners malfunctioned and left oily soot on the barn of tobacco.

Once the tobacco was colored as good as possible it was time to go up on the heat. Going up on the heat or drying the stems was the final curing process. It required a higher heat of about 175 degrees. It took about two days to bake all the moisture from the stems. It was also a more dangerous part of the process. However, once the stems were dried of all moisture the heat could be turned off and the cooling time begun. It was a general rule of thumb that you filled the barn and seven days later removed the tobacco and refilled it. When it was time to turn off the heat the doors were opened and the small windows in the top of the barn were opened as well for more airflow. If the heat was turned off during the daylight hours and a warm and humid night followed the tobacco could be removed the next morning without it crumbling due to its being too dry.

Curing was a twenty-four-hour job. In order to keep a constant eye on what was happening and also to help prevent falling leaves from catching on fire the barn was checked about every four *hours. It was the last thing you did before going to sleep and often what you did during the middle of the night. It was the first thing you did when you woke up. And, it was what you did all through the day. The farmer was constantly looking for when to set the color and when to run up on the heat. It was a constant concern on the farmer's mind.*

My father had three barns, two four-room barns and one five-room barn. We knew that we would be filling them each week. He also sharecropped two other farms. He was cash-renting the tobacco poundage. The tobacco was allotted to each farm at so many pounds for the farm. It was tracked by the pound when selling and allotted by the pound to each farm by the government. A farmer could rent his poundage annually to another farmer who shouldered the cost of growing it and kept whatever profit was left. He would have to farm a certain amount of the land on the farm holding the tobacco poundage, which may or may not be the tobacco crop. The poundage was converted into acreage when planted. Each farm had an expected yield per acre and you were only allowed to plant the number of acres that met the poundage. You could sell ten percent over your poundage but it was deducted from next year's crop.

Growing up I remember traveling to the two different farms week after week and using the barns on those farms to cure the tobacco. It wasn't until bulk barns were available, in my High School years, that enough curing space was available to grow the entire acreage on Daddy's farm.

By the time I was old enough to drive the tractor Daddy had purchased a harvester that was made for four croppers and stringers and had a place to hold the sticks of tobacco until you reached the end of the row. Shortly afterward we started using just two croppers and using half of the harvester. We were able to use just two croppers and still fill one barn a day. Many farmers, by using four croppers and a drag, were able to fill two barns in a day. Daddy had become very frustrated with locating and caring for additional helpers and decided to keep the workers to family and close friends. When I began High School the need for more income forced Daddy to increase the acreage and return to four croppers. He purchased three bulk barns. Each bulk barn would cure twice the amount of conventional barns. When problems again arose with maintaining the help needed to harvest the crop, he turned to a harvester that mounted on the tractor and stripped the stalk of all the leaves as it passed. The advantage of the striper and bulk barns was that the help was greatly reduced and the tobacco harvested in one day still remained about the same.

Year after year the summer routine centered around the hoeing, suckering, topping, cropping and grading of the tobacco. The grading began for me as a tedious work and by the time I left the farm after college was virtually non-existent. My first memories of grading tobacco were of a work Daddy oversaw and personally did. As already mentioned, the cured tobacco had to be taken to the packhouse. It was stacked there until we were able, on the days that we were not gathering, to remove it from the sticks and prepare it for market. The process began with taking the sticks of tobacco from the top floor of a two-story barn down to the ground floor to be hung over night to better soften it. The tedious part started the next day.

Our packhouses were a mule barn and the old milk barn. We did most of our work in the milk barn due to the coolness from the concrete floor and because it helped in softening the tobacco. The tobacco was kept on the upper floors that were used for storing hay during the fall and winter. We would all gather for the event, even the infants. The children too young to work were kept in a homemade playpen. First the sticks of tobacco were unsewed of the tobacco. The sticks were held by a homemade grip on a wall stud or pole. We also had a couple of homemade holders that were freestanding and extended upward about waist high with two notches for the two ends of the stick to rest in. To remove the tobacco the string would be broken at one end of the stick and then each handful of the tobacco had to be grasped and pulled away from the stick allowing the string to unwind itself. When your hands were full or your arms became too short to pull the tobacco free of *the ever-lengthening twine, you would take it to a table where the graders were.*

The graders were generally daddy and sometimes an uncle who was familiar with the various grades and what the buyers would be wanting. The grading process was for removing any unwanted leaves and grouping the leaves in preset grades. Once the tobacco was separated into the various grades the tying began. The tobacco was gathered into bundles that you could barely grip your hand around and then wrapped with a special leaf put aside just for tying the handful of tobacco leaves. The many handfuls were then placed on special grading sticks, much more slender than the others and also worn slick by the routine sliding of the tobacco on them, and readied for the warehouse. When taken to the warehouse to be sold they were there transferred to a basket in a circular manner with the stems toward the outside of the basket. The tobacco would be stacked about thigh high and placed in rows. The next day the buyers from the many cigarette companies would walk down the rows in groups and bid against each other for the piles of tobacco. Each grade had an expected price and what was bid was usually pretty close to the expected price.

As the years passed the tying gradually faded away and the tobacco was placed on burlap sheets with the loose stems facing out and the sheet tied until placed on the warehouse floor. The grading continued until I was out of grammar school. By then the tobacco was scanned by hand for ugly leaves and swollen, or undried stems, and made clean and more appealing for the buyers. With the coming of bulk barns and the mixing of grades by striping, harvesting all the leaves on the stalk at one time, and cropping more leaves at the time the tobacco was simply stuffed in a round form that sat on burlap sheets and tied until placed on a row in the warehouse. The sheets were to hold 200 to 250 pounds of tobacco.

The market generally opened in early to mid July. That meant that come the middle of July the average farmer was focused on gathering, curing and getting the tobacco ready for market. That is when you walk on eggshells around the farm. You can see the stress and anxiety on each farmer's face. The first relief comes when the farmer puts his first load of tobacco on the warehouse floor and gets his first check of the season. That brings a little relief but much of the season still remains.

Tobacco gathering continues until the crop is out of the field. That may happen in August or sometimes not until September. There have been a few times, generally due to the lack of barn space for gathering the tobacco more quickly, that tobacco gathering was still going on after school started. That was not until the first of September back in those days and normally not until after Labor Day. I remember many times that for weeks and even a month after starting school we would spend our afternoons and early evenings after returning home taking the tobacco off the sticks and preparing it for market. By the time the tobacco was sold and those to whom we were indebted were satisfied it was October.

For the farmer the sale of his crop wasn't the end of the season. In order to use the land for another year the woody stalks had to be cut down and turned into the soil where they would decay and enrich the soil for another planting. The tractor made this much easier. I always enjoyed coming home from school and getting on the tractor with the rotary mower, or Bush Hog as one manufacturer named their product, and mowing down those symbols of the long, demanding and tiring days of summer. Next came the disc that sliced the stalks and tossed the soil turning all weeds, grass and stalks underground. You could disc the rows and see the roots of the stalks turned up. This was left for most of the fall and early winter awaiting the decaying of the root system and stalks. The fall rains were a great help in their decaying.

The warehouse was always a treat for the younger farmers. There were rows and rows of tobacco sheets. The smell was so concentrated that you could detect it for blocks away from the warehouse. I always enjoyed the smell and even today passing a warehouse and getting a whiff of the smell brings back these and many other memories. Our trips to the warehouse were marked by two pleasures shared by many of the adults too.

The first was a snokone. It was a cone cup filled with crushed ice and a deliciously sweet flavoring added atop. It brought coolness to the hot summer days and much pleasure to little and big taste buds.

The second treat was the familiar rhythmic cry of, "Peanuts, Peanuts, two for a quarter." The quarter's value shrank over the years but the enjoyment of eating boiled peanuts never faded. The small brown paper bags were filled most of the way and the top was rolled down and the two corners twisted tightly holding the peanuts in the bag. Almost anywhere on the warehouse floor you could see peanut hulls. If you were really lucky the salty boiled peanuts would be finished off with a cold Pepsi Cola. Otherwise, you just had to get a drink of cold water from the water fountain.

The warehouse was usually a happy place. Sometimes the farmers were disappointed with the price their crop brought. Most often the farmers were elated to finally be getting some return for the previous eight to ten months of work and relieved at the prospects of paying off some of their annual debts. Needless to say, the bankers were usually present and looking quite happy too.

When the tobacco was finally sold and the debts paid, the year was still not over. The cutting of the stalks, the putting away of the equipment, the cleaning of the barns and a million other little clean-up jobs kept the farmer busy. That led to the harvesting of the corn crop that generally came toward the end of October or first of November. For the farming family November was a special month. Thanksgiving was a holiday with special significance. Each farmer was thankful for another year and for the crops now harvested that led to another year of opportunity. This was a season for joyful thankfulness. It was also the least busy time for the farmer and hunting was a common way of getting away from the months of demanding strain on the farmers.

Five

Backer Time Fun

In the 1940's this barn was used for Meadowlawn Dairy. The cows were milked in the barn and the milk pumped to the two-room building beside it for processing and bottling. After closing the dairy, the barn was the main processing place for tobacco. After being cured, the tobacco was softened, un-strung, graded, tied and made ready for the warehouse for sale. The cement floor helped with the softening, or moisturizing, and was much appreciated as a place to work. The two lower doors would be opened, and a wonderful breeze would most always flow through the work area. It also served for storing hay in the winter.

It seems that most of the memories of the many fun things enjoyed as a child naturally occurred around tobacco gathering time. In the spring when the clock was turned forward for Daylight Savings time and the icy chill of winter passes it was time to work the tobacco beds and plant the fields. As school days came to a close and all-day freedom returned it was time to harvest and then make ready the tobacco for the market until the school days return. Most of the fun took place in or around the continuing work of planting, harvesting and selling the tobacco crop.

Living on a farm offered many opportunities that I enjoyed and still miss even today, decades later. The farm was a place to explore. As a young child my older sisters and I would leave the grassy yard for the wooded perimeters to explore and play in a make-believe world. It may be constructing forts from limbs and pieces of wood scavenged from the woods or riding the western frontier of the Indians, but the woods were a magical place. One of our favorite spots was actually on our neighbor's farm just north of us. A small ditch separated our properties. On our neighbor's side were mounds of dirt that formed the ditch bank on their side and the wooded area was narrow and open. We could play and still see my grandmother's house through the wooded area and our house just beyond it. Many days we would run and play in these woods and enjoy the mounds of dirt that were transformed into many things by our imagination.

The empty tobacco barns were also great places to explore. The doors never had locks but only simple latches, a piece of wood attached to the door frame with a single nail that allowed the small piece of wood to be turned and hold the wooden door shut. Being closed and dark all year kept grass and weeds from growing in the barns. The annual curing of tobacco also left a layer of sand on the barn floor that was great for digging and constructing roads and having great fun in the dirt. When we grew tired of playing in the dirt, we could always climb the tier poles. It was always fun to challenge our fears and climb to the top of the barn and push open the small solid wooden window for an amazing look at the farm from about twenty-five feet up.

I remember doing something similar at my uncle's house across the highway. He was into ham radios and had erected a tower for his antenna that was taller than the pine trees all around his home. One day while visiting my cousins I faced my fearful hesitations and slowly climbed to the top. It was a most beautiful and frightening experience. I had no ropes or safety equipment, just a firm grip and week knees. I arose to the top of the pine trees and looked over the two ponds, which now looked rather small beside our seemingly small house. I looked at the farm on which I had walked, worked and played. It was a moving moment of beauty. Then there was the fearful journey back down the tower. Thankfully I returned to earth without any harm.

The farm was a place to roam but roaming can be dangerous. Once when the family was gathering tobacco on another farm closer to town and my oldest sister was home babysitting my youngest sister, we returned and soon realize that my youngest sister wasn't to be found in either the house or the yard. My mother was deathly afraid of water and always feared her children drowning in the ponds. She just knew that my youngest sister had gone to the ponds and would be found drowned. We began a massive search. Like the trackers in the movies, we searched for footprints and any sign of which direction her little footprints might have gone. Soon her footprints were found going not toward the ponds but down the dirt road to the fields. That had its dangers too. There were tractors, heavy equipment, poisons, snakes and a host of other dangers. Mom was not comforted by that direction either. The search party made its way toward the barns and began calling her name and looking under and around everything. The first two barns were about an eight of a mile from the house. She was nowhere to be found.

Someone located the footprints leaving the barns and going further into the field. About a quarter of a mile from the house were the furthest barns. The oldest was a log barn no longer used and beside it was a newer barn constructed in the forties. It had no shelter around it and therefore was a constant source of complaints when we harvested tobacco and had to work in the direct sunlight, and rain. The search party quickly made its way to the furthest barn with prayers and held breaths. As they reached the barn calling her name and hoping for a miracle of grace, they found it. She was there at the barn safe and only scared. She had wondered from the house and being undetected wandered into the fields in search of her mother and father, thinking them to be at work in the fields. The party returned home in much joy and many flowing tears offering prayers of thanksgiving.

One of the fun things I always enjoyed was the opportunity to ride on the tractor with my father. I would often see him in the field plowing, disking or working with the tractor and make my way in hopes of a free ride. I can remember on many occasions riding at his side. I would sometimes find myself growing sleepy and would fall across his lap into a sleep brought on by the warmth from the tractor's motor and the constant sound of its running. I found it very interesting just standing beside the tractor seat and looking back at the equipment being pulled behind the tractor.

Just before starting grammar school, I had a great uncle that lived about a quarter of a mile up the road. He would often walk the railroad tracks in front of our houses to visit his sister, my grandmother, who lived next door to us. I can only *recall a few memories about him but they are all pleasant memories of his time and attention given me. He was too frail to work and now had plenty of time to sit with children and tell them the many stories of years gone by. He also shared ways that he had used in his childhood to entertain himself and even some that got him into trouble. One was making a whistle out of a reed. There were many reeds growing along the ditch banks on the farm. One day while talking with me he asked me if I knew how to make a whistle from a reed. I of course said no and he asked me to run and cut a reed. I brought it back and he took his pocketknife and cut a section from the larger end of the reed. He cut the section leaving one end closed with the joint and the other open cutting it just before the second joint. He then cut a small notch near the open end and handed it to me. I blew in it but it made no noise. He laughed and said it wasn't finished yet. He then took a little stick and whittled it so it would slide into the reed tightly. The small wooden piece had a flat side cut on it so that the flat side fit under the notch. He adjusted it to just the right length and gave it back to me. "Blow now," he said. I did and it made a whistling sound. That was my first reed whistle. Since then I have made a large box full of them.*

One of his entertainment pieces that got him in trouble was a reed popgun. First, he cut a section of the reed removing both joint sections making it a hollow tube. Second, he cut a smaller section that would slide loosely into the tube and cut a small section that would go on one end of the smaller plunging piece so as to give you a larger end to firmly hit with the palm of your hand. The plunger was shortened so as to go almost all the way down the tube. Once the tube and the plunger were completed it was time to get the ammunition. The ammunition was black cherries. When the black cherries are green, they are small and firm. The first cherry was forced into the tube and pushed down just short of coming out the other end. Then the second cherry was placed in the tube and barely pushed into the tube. The theory is that the second cherry will create enough air pressure when forced down the tube quickly to explode the first cherry out the other end. The second cherry now remains in the barrel for your second shot. The cherries wouldn't cause any serious injury but would be similar to shooting each other with a BB gun. As you can imagine the shooter would have much fun but those shot would not always see it as fun. When the parents got involved, the shooting wasn't fun anymore.

He came regularly and I always looked forward to spending time with him. Not long afterward I found out that he had died. It seems that he went to bed one night and never woke up. I have often thought how blessed he was to have had relatively good health and to peacefully die in his sleep without all the long and painful journey of illness and suffering.

From time to time, we would have members of our extended family stop by for a week or several days to visit with Grandmother and Granddaddy. They called it a vacation. I always thought of vacation as being our summer out of school. I can only remember one time being far enough away from home that we spent the night. That was a time when we were visiting my mother's sister near Raleigh N.C. Daddy had agreed to lay some floor covering for her and it gave us a unique experience of being away from home over night. Daddy was quite content, however, to stay on the farm and always saw the many responsibilities, feeding the cows, dogs and being sure the cattle stayed in the fences, as good enough reasons to stay at home. A vacation for us was going to Boy Scout camp for me and going to other summer camps for my sisters. Summer was a time for work and until the work began the children vacationed by playing and exploring the farm. As already mentioned, farming wasn't a lucrative business. Family vacations were usually expensive outings. Part of farming was being very thrifty and denying yourself so as to continue the privilege of farming the land and livestock. As a result, summer was filled with hoeing, working the tobacco, getting in the hay, keeping the electric fences flowing with electricity so the cows wouldn't get out and more. There were a million reasons not to take a vacation. So we just didn't.

Another favorite activity of fun was catching lightening bugs, or fireflies as they are called. In the early summer months with the singing of the tree frogs came the nighttime greenish sparkles of the lightening bugs. When my cousins came for a visit, it was a great time to collect these mysterious creatures that created flashes of light. We would get glass jars with metal lids that had holes punched in them by an ice pick. We would run across the yard in the dark grabbing at the tiny flashing lights. Once caught, they were put into the jar with some grass and kept under the closed lid. Invariable we would bring them into the house and you guessed it, let them escape to entertain us when the lights went out.

With the passing of the summer heat and the return of school came another time of great fun. It was the town fair. The town fair was a mix, though quickly fading mix, of an agricultural fair and entertainment fair. There were many rides of all kinds. Most of which would make those with a weak equilibrium quickly sick, of which I was one. There weren't many rides that I could handle. The quick tossing and turning was more than my equilibrium could tolerate. So at an early age I learned to avoid the different rides so those sitting beside or behind me wouldn't get their ride ruined.

The fair was held at the old farmers market. I went to the market a time or two with my father who once took a chance at farming pole beans. We took the baskets to the market to sell them. During the fall, about October, we would return for the fair. There would be various judged events like quilts, canned foods, a few cattle, pigs or other animals, and many displays of tractors or things of interest to the farmer.

However, the real excitement was outside the large warehouse building. We would usually have to enter the building and make our way to the large back door that led to a world filled with children's fantasies. There were games everywhere that beckoned you to try your hand at winning a tempting prize for just a quarter. You could walk the long walkways lined with games of luck and displaying all kinds of stuffed animals that could be won. There was cotton candy for sale, candied apples, popcorn and all the unhealthy things your mother didn't want you to eat. And then there was the houchie couchie shows. That was where the girls, barely dressed, came out and danced inviting the men to pay up and enter the tent for a real show. Needless to say, it was the topic of much preaching by ministers and every boy's mother. However, many fathers didn't listen to their mother or their wife and found themselves among the eyeing crowd. It was always the topic of conversation at the schoolyard. And there were always the boys that said they snuck inside and told of the real show with many descriptive words.

If it had not been for the county school system we would not have gone to the fair. On Friday of the week of the town fair schools let out about mid-morning and bused all the children to the fairgrounds. Our parents would meet us there and the day was filled with spending money on rides, games and food, that wonderful unhealthy stuff. After the money was spent and the tummies were disturbed with unaccustomed exploitations, the weary and worn would make their way back to the familiar comforts of home. If you were lucky, you could take home a stuffed toy won at one of the games or for some a ribbon awarded for their superior entry. By Monday morning the rides, games and much of our town's money were all gone and our little town returned to its routines.

When I was in high school, my two best friends and I stumbled onto an idea. I cannot remember just how it came about but it arose and we decided to go for it. One of my two high school companions worked with his mother each summer running a Putt-Putt golf course at the beach. They had a cotton candy machine, popcorn machine and all that was needed to make candied apples. It was suggested that we turn the fair to our advantage by making a small business venture. We paid a small fee to rent a booth in the warehouse and purchased some apples along with the supplies to make popcorn, cotton candy and provide Pepsis and Cokes. We spent each afternoon and evening manning the booth and selling our products to the many people who came by. It was a week of excitement as we saw our investment prosper. By Saturday night when the machines were loaded and the booth left vacant, we gathered to count the proceeds. Three kids were ecstatic when they realized that the profit would come to well over a hundred dollars each. That was a significant chunk of change in the early seventies.

Like many things it started as a simple way to add a little fun to the daily work routine. Who thought up the idea is no longer known. All I can remember were the many days of laughter and friendly competition that added much fun and occasional bright spots in an otherwise demanding and sweltering hot workday.

It began as an idea to make something like a chariot. On the farm there are usually many spare parts to broken toys and objects discarded from days gone bye but not thrown away. It is with a mind of imagination that these objects come together and something eventful begins. And thus began the tobacco chariot race.

We were gathering tobacco with the harvester. No, this was before the present-day tobacco combines. Our harvester was a metal framed contraption which was pulled behind the slowest tractor and allowed four people to crop, four to string the tobacco on sticks and a ninth person to place the strung sticks on a small platform until reaching the end of the row. We were only using two croppers and stringers and would make a complete round before unloading the sticks of tobacco neatly lain on the platform. At the end of a round we would transfer the sticks to a large wooden trailer

and after about eight rounds or so carry the sticks
to the barn for hanging before returning to do it
all over again. I, and my cousins from across the
road, except the two older girls who had married
and moved away, were junior high to high school
age. We were the farm workforce along with my
sisters. So as our creative and always wandering
minds stumbled across an idea to make chariots,
we naturally went to work on it. Daddy's custom
of taking a nap after lunch gave time to work on
our plan. Each morning and each day after lunch,
we would ride to the field on the large wooden
trailer, used for transporting the sticks of strung
tobacco, to work. We would all get on the trailer
to ride to the barn several times each day and
back to the field as well. We decided to add a little
excitement by making use of several items lying
around the farm.

Tobacco sticks were plentiful as well as the heavy
twine used for holding the bails of hay together.
Also, there were several metal milk bottle crates
that were about the same size as the plastic milk
jug crates seen in grocery stores today. The last
essential element was the metal axles from
discarded wagons and tricycles. We ran the axles
through the edge of the open end of the metal
crates that left the bottom, now the top, as our flat
surface for sitting. The tobacco stick was tied to
the crate and then attached to the back of the
trailer and the chariots were ready to ride.
Usually, Daddy went rather slowly to the field as

some sat and others stood for the ride. Now with
two, and sometimes three, nuts sitting on milk
crate chariots itching to fall off, the temptation
was just too great. He would give the tractor the
gas and as the small chariot hit a hole in the road,
we would naturally go flying one way or the other.
We would roll from the fall and our observers
would roll from laughter. Sometimes the bailing
twine would become worn or work loose and either
the crate would come loose from the stick and over
we and our chariot would go or the stick would
come loose from the trailer and over we would go
as the stick suddenly stopped the chariot but not
us. This went on for a week or two and then it was
time for some modifications.

We always looked forward to lunch. The hard
work made us all hungry and the food was a
special pleasure in a day of great demands. But
after lunch we looked forward to Daddy's routine
nap. Daddy has always taken a nap after lunch.
We certainly never complained but enjoyed the
hour or so relaxing under the shade of the pecan
trees, down here we say Pee-can. It was these
daily naptimes that turned us into mid-day pit
crews quickly adjusting and modifying our latest
designs for the afternoon runs. We decided that
we could take a board, about eight to ten inches
wide and around four or five feet in length, and
turn it into a flat-bed tobacco derby vehicle. We
nailed the axles from the chariots on the back and
found another to use up front. We had to be able

to steer so we took a small narrow board for the front that was just long enough to fit between the front wheels. With the axle firmly attached to it we then ran a single nail through the center of it and through the front center of the large board. We first used our feet to push the front axle and steer the cart. We then tied bailing twine to the axle and could steer by pulling one side or the other. The only problem was that when the twine rubbed against the wheels it would wear through and we would go flying as the cart turned out of control.

At first the fun was in just riding the carts and trying to control them enough to stay on them. It was kind of like riding a wild bronco. As we were learning the art of steering and balancing ourselves, Daddy was developing an art of speeding up and slowing down, which made our mastering of the ride more difficult. Once we finally mastered the ride, we discovered that if we swung over and came up behind the other cart, our wheel would rise up over theirs and throw us off our cart. However, if we would swing over and get our wheel in from of theirs, they would rise up over our wheel and roll off their cart. With that a new competition was begun. Several times daily the fun was on. The mounting of our tobacco derby carts and the chess match of who stays on and who gets thrown off brought a new anticipation to our workday. This was the only time that my father actually put the tractor in its higher gear to look *back and see the swerving and tumbling carts behind him.*

Part of mastering the carts was the art of stopping them. We had no brakes so our feet were all we had to use. Our carts were attached to the trailer with a rope. When the tractor stopped, we had two choices: plant our feet and stop before running under the trailer or bail off and let the cart fend for itself. Usually, we were able to stop but, occasionally we had to ditch our vehicle and repair any damages later in the garage.

There was one other danger, the electric fence posts. These posts were creosote post about four inches in diameter. From time to time, we found ourselves unable to avoid contact with one of these unmovable objects and as a result major work was ahead for the pit crew during lunch. Thankfully no one was seriously hurt. But many lasting memories were made and a few laughs still rise from within when recalling these memories.

When earlier and still in the blessed innocent years, those childhood years in which you were excused from the workload, I enjoyed a sort of fishing thing. We would go across the road in front of our house toward the middle of summer. It was to unstring, grade and prepare the tobacco for the market. While my parents and others worked inside the barn, I would make my way to a large drainage ditch that ran parallel to the highway. We called it a canal because of its size. It was wide enough that only a few were able to jump across it. It was also about six or seven feet deep at the crossing. When large rains came it would be full of water until the water could cross under the road just beyond the barn and flow down our property line to the creek running behind the farm. There was almost always water in the ditch.

One day while investigating the running water in the bottom of the ditch I discovered an interesting crustacean crawling along the muddy bottom. It was what we knew as crawdads, or crawfish. They were miniature fresh water lobsters, very miniature. Their size was seldom more than two or three inches. Their tiny claws were still able to give an unwanted pinch. So the question became, "How do I catch one of these things?"

Having played and pillaged around the barn I had run into several usable items. There was plenty of used tobacco twine that could be doubled or braided to make a strong twine. The old barn was a dairy barn run by my father in the forties and fifties. Scattered around were different sizes of glass milk bottles. The string was tied just below the lip on the milk bottle and lowered gently near a scavenging crawdad. Then there was the wait, and watch, watch and wait and cat-like excitement as the crawdad began inching its way near the mouth of the submerged bottle. And then as the curious crustacean made his way into the bottle, I pulled the string lifting the bottle by its mouth and capturing the crawdad in a clear but secure prison. Sometimes the wait was too long and I would just leave my crawdad trap in the water and return later to seize my underwater victim.

The thrill of catching one was really more fun than playing with them. They were fun to hold and watch as they tried to get their pinchers around to your fingers as they were held by their shrimp like tail. Every once in a while, they managed to succeed and you would, in fright and surprise, react by shaking your hand and slinging them flying through the air where you would need to once more go through the quick and careful maneuvering needed to grab them without getting pinched again. Usually, the crawdads were put back into the water. There were never many of them and eating them wasn't a real consideration. They were just living play toys that helped pass the fleeting days of summer as I awaited my introduction into the routine farm workforce.

Another fun activity came during the hay season. If you fertilized well and had good rainfall you could usually get three cuttings of hay a year. The first came in the late spring or early summer. The hay was first cut with an old cycle mower that was around at my earliest memories. The mower was attached to the back of the tractor and had a seven-foot blade that worked much like hedge trimmers. Daddy would go round and around the field cutting a six-foot swipe of the coastal Bermuda grass

A horse drawn mower.

to dry for bailing several days later.

Hay was an essential for the cows that needed food in the winter. We had pastures that grew grass up until a hard freeze. But during the coldest months of winter, and until the grass was plentiful in the spring, the main source of food for the herd of twenty plus cows was hay, and lots of it. Cows were not a big money-making venture. To buy hay reduced what little profit could be made so growing your own hay helped increase a little cash flow. The process was simple. First you cut the field of grass used for hay. Usually, a particular type was planted and nurtured that would give the cows nutrition and an incentive to eat it, other than just hunger. The coastal Bermuda hay was one the cows would come to eat even in the summer. Next the cut hay lay on the ground one or two days for drying. Then it was raked into large rows and left another day to be sure what was underneath is dry. The importance of drying is to prevent any moisture from starting the rotting process once packed and stacked in the barn. The next day the hay was raked once more, after the dew was completely dry, and shortly after lunch the bailing, hauling and stacking began.

That, as you can imagine, wasn't the fun part. The fun part came during the mowing. In the knee-high hay field were many nesting creatures, birds of various kinds and rabbits. Yes, rabbits were fun. As the mower came close to the rabbit's nest or shallow den the rabbits, little and large, would run in fear, which was smart considering the mower's inability to distinguish between animal and vegetation. The yard dogs were always present and anxious for the chase. Sometimes, one or two of us children were present and awaiting a chase too. The large rabbits were of course too fast. However, the little ones were not so quick and hadn't developed their endurance yet.

The mower would come upon a rabbit's home and out would run several rabbits. We would look for the little ones and try to beat the dogs to them, who had other intentions for them if caught. The larger rabbits would run off and we would, after much running, twisting, turning and going around in circles, finally corner a tired and scared rabbit. After a few minutes the rabbit would catch its breath and lose some of its fearfulness in our gentle, yet secure grip. We would then head for the house to build a rabbit pen.

It may be an old fish aquarium, cardboard box, or some other such container, but we found something that would contain the little rabbit and protect him from the very interested cats. We would find a metal or wire lid for the box that allowed for plenty of air. We would gather grass and, of course, carrots which everybody knew rabbits eat. We would get a small can that could be filled with water. Then we would put our rabbit pen on the front porch since momma wouldn't let rabbits in the house.

However, our rabbits usually never remained more than a day or two. No, we gave them plenty of water and food. The problem we were to learn was that the cats, which showed such an interest in our little pets, used the unprotected nighttime hours to find a way of getting these little furry creatures for their late-night snack. On several occasions we arose the next morning to find only a bit of fur and an empty box. The cats on the other hand greeted us warmly and with grins on their faces.

Six

SNAKES!!!

The two barns where the rattlesnake was found.

What better place to discover the world of snakes than on a farm? You were out among the wildlife, working the fields and moving equipment stored around barns that sat vacant most of the year. Even the mule barn where corn was stored for feeding was a place to see snakes. For some this would be a great opportunity to investigate and get a close look at the "no shoulder" buggers as we often referred to them. But for others it was a continual experience of heart failure and uncontrolled muscle reflexes. Mine was the latter.

Whether a person is born with certain fears or later learns them I do not know. What I do know is that, once you are afraid, it is next to impossible to conquer that fear. My mother was deathly afraid of water and snakes. I remember once, as a young child, my mother standing inside the back door of the house and shouting, "Children, there's a snake in the backyard!" I of course went to investigate with wobbling knees. I looked over the grassy yard in search of a long snake coiled or on the move. It had been rainy and the grass was wet. I thought perhaps a snake had been under one of the many doghouses and was run out by the water. Instead, my mother pointed to a bare place where we burned our trash. It was another good place. Once or twice a year we would get the tractor and trailer and fork the cans and non-burnable trash onto the trailer and haul it to the woods for nature's recycling program. Mice would sometimes be seen in the warmer months around such a treasured place for raising a family and foraging food. Black snakes or other kinds of snakes would come in search of a meal of their own. But I couldn't see a black snake, chicken snake, pilot snake, copper head or other undesirable no-legged creature. Mom insisted with panic in her voice that a snake was wiggling and twisting on the wet dirt surface.

I squeezed between her and the screen door and made my way cautiously out to the area. Perhaps there was a small snake that had been hatched under the trash pile and others might be present too. As I approached the bare spot, I saw a wiggling and twisting eelworm, we called them, squirming to cover itself. An eelworm was a large brown worm that was particularly hyperactive for a worm. The earthworm was a dark blue or almost black worm of similar size. We would dig earthworms for fishing but found the eelworms to be troublesome to put on a hook and undesirable for the fish. I laughed and tried to convince my mother that what she saw was just a worm. Needless to say, it was a futile effort. For my mother, if it didn't have shoulders or legs, it was suspect. If it was long and moved by wiggling and twisting it was a snake, small, large or otherwise. My mother never thought of a snake as being helpful or friendly. It was always the enemy of Eve and womanhood. It was to be destroyed, by someone else of course, and removed from our earthly experience.

As you might imagine, living on the farm was a lifelong trial for mom. It was often a cardiovascular workout for me too. Once I went into daddy's tool shed. I often went into it to beat and bang on some project. That day as I went into the shed I, for some unusual reason turned to look back at the doorway. Draped across the top of the doorframe lay a long chicken snake. Now my heart was pounding and my feet were jumping up and down and my arms were trying to decide which way my body was going to go so they wouldn't be left behind. I wished I could say that what took place next was an act of bravery. However, the truth is that staying in the tool shed meant staying with the snake and going through the door meant risking his falling on me, which of course would mean a sure heart attack and a funeral for the family. In an unconscious and unpremeditated act, I flung my body through the door and never looked back until far out into the yard. That event changed the way I entered the tool shed for many years.

Snakeskins were a common find on the farm. Almost every year when we would go into the loft of the mule barn or the milk barn, we would find a long snakeskin shed from the previous year's growth. Daddy would ascend into the loft to push and sweep away the hay left from the winter's feeding. We put the tobacco from the barn into the loft to store it until it could be graded and sheeted for the market. As Daddy would sweep away the hay and move some of the objects stored, he would usually come across a skin shed by a slithering barn dweller. He would bring it to us and we would hold it and think of what its former owner looked like and just where he might be. Needless to say, we always went into the loft of the barns with an expectant eye for snakes. Seldom, however, did we actually see one. By summer the mice were out in the fields and woods foraging for food. And, so were the snakes, who welcomed joining one for lunch.

I recall one particular incident when we were gathering tobacco. We were working at the double barns. The double barns were two tobacco barns, a five-room and a four-room barn, which were about thirty feet apart. A shelter had been built which connected the two barns and extended across the front of both and around the side of the one closest to the house. This shelter allowed much needed space for storing the tractors, trailers, hay bailer and other valued but idled farm implements. We were at the four-room barn. The drags were brought under the shelter and the stringing was done right at the barn's door. Just beside the work area, between the two barns, was where the tractor was kept and just beyond it toward the back of the barn was the hay bailer. It was a dirt area with usual clutter. While working someone noticed a snake under the bailer. With a holler and a yell, the snake alarm was sounded and everyone sprang into action. I was only a child working around the drag but I acted with quickness and decisiveness. I ran out from under the shelter and stood outside looking. My mother had been stringing. When the alarm sounded, she disappeared. When I regained my senses, I looked toward the house and saw my mother going into the house an eighth of a mile away. She had run all the way to the house fleeing what she knew was certain death, in many ways of course. It was my grandfather who had the calmness to grab a pitchfork leaning against the barn and to pin the snake to the ground and then finish killing it. When it was dead, he brought it out hanging limply over the prongs of the pitchfork. I had been taught that dead snakes are like discarded poison, dangerous and deadly. In this case it was true for the snake was a rattler. For the rest of the day, we jumped at every sound and could hardly work for snake watching. Mom spent the rest of the day at the house, returning to the snake pit wasn't an option for her that day.

My father still laughs about the time two of his brothers went fishing. Fishing was always an enjoyable time away from the pressing work of the farm. Our farm was about half way between the Little Pee Dee and the Waccamaw rivers. With the onslaught of automobiles, the ten to twelve mile trip became much shorter. When an opportunity to take a break and head off to the river came, the boat and paddles were quickly grabbed, and a few worms were dug and it was off to the fishing hole with a cane pole in hand. My uncles reached the river and readied for what they hoped would be a productive fishing day. In those days fishing wasn't just for fun. You didn't hear of people in expensive boats using the "catch and release" method. The old method was "catch and eat!" Fishing, though an enjoyable time away, was also a way to supplement the family diet. With that in mind a fishing trip would be capped off by *bringing home some tasty fish to add further enjoyment to the family at suppertime.*

Bringing home a catch was an important male ego thing. No fisherman wants to return home empty handed. The family knows you left and when you arrive home they will have the frying pan in hand awaiting a fresh change to the daily dietary menu. Once a couple of my uncles decided to go to the river fishing, but found the day to be unproductive. Being smart and unwilling to suffer the indignity of returning home empty handed, they decided to stop by the fish market. They chose several nice fish and returned home smiling. They brought the fish to my grandmother and bragged of their successful trip. My grandmother smiled back and said, "Son these are nice fish, but I thought you were going to the river not the ocean." They had unknowingly purchased saltwater fish.

This day was not to be noted for a mistaken catch. Paddling around the overhanging limbs was where you would find the fish. The fish are around the many obstacles along the banks of the river and not in the center clearing. So, a good fisherman knows how to maneuver his boat around and under the overhanging tree limbs to fish around the stumps and roots and shallow bedding areas. The limbs pose two problems for the fisherman. First, they seem to reach out and grab the line on your pole. I was often accused of fishing for squirrels instead of fish because of my continual fighting with the tree limbs. The other was a more

dangerous problem, snakes. The snakes would feed
in the water and being cold blooded would seek a
warm place to replenish their body heat in the
sun. As a result, you might ease up near a limb
and discover that you had eased under a
sunbathing snake. Most were harmless, as far as
the bite goes, water snakes. However, every
Southerner fears the infamous water moccasin.
The water moccasin is a highly poisonous snake
that is territorial and will actually defend its
claim. For this reason, they have been the source
of every fisherman's fear and the cause of death
for so many more species of snakes along the
river. Many fishermen carried a firearm with them
and any snake was considered a moccasin and
thus an expendable enemy of society.

Usually, the sunbathing snake would drop from
the limb and dive under the water to escape the
approaching unknown creature. Sometimes they
would swim on top of the water and even come
close to the boat. That is what took place with my
uncles. The snake swam right up to the boat. One
of my uncles was deathly afraid of snakes and
decided to prevent the snake from coming into the
boat by breaking his little neck if he could. He
quickly grabbed the paddle and began beating the
water in hopes of killing the snake. What
happened next is uncertain. Whether the snake
wanted a look inside the boat or whether my uncle
actually hit the snake and slung him into the boat
with the flying paddle is not known. What is

known is that the snake came into the boat and two men found that sharing a small boat with a crawling and quickly moving snake was not their idea of a pleasant fishing experience. Now two paddles went flying. For miles down the river you could have heard two men shouting and shuffling in the small boat and beating the boat with their paddles in hopes of killing the snake and removing him from their presence. As they swung their paddles the paddles began turning to splinters. It only took a minute for the snake to see all he wanted to see in the boat. He finally found the way over the side of the boat and back into the water. As my uncles tried to slow their hearts and regain their composure, they discovered that their paddles had been reduced to toothpicks and their mode of propulsion greatly reduced. It was a story told many times and a reminder to let swimming snakes swim on by.

Another of the memorable snake experiences came one spring. As mentioned, we had a large recycling station just beyond the hedgerow of the field. On the backside of the farm was an area where the terrain dropped about four of five feet just past the tree line. It was a natural place to put discarded furniture, wooden items and metal items for the slow process of returning to differing minerals in the soil. From time to time, I would stop by the dumping place to pillage through the discarded items. One spring, when the trees had just put out leaves and the grass was growing fast and green, I decided to take a look at the dump. I made my way to the back of the field and eased through the bushes that strained toward the field in hopes of getting sunlight. There was so much debris from the many years of discarded trash that I walked onto the pile that was almost level with the field. I took about six steps and looked over the back of the pile to what lay discarded at the bottom. My eye noticed something just over to my left and when I look again my heart stopped. It was a copperhead coiled and angry. He was about three or four feet from me. I looked to my right thinking I could move away from him in that direction, but saw another coiled and watching. I was now ready to vacate the premises and forget the idea. The only problem was that were three other smaller snakes coiled between my exit and me. I couldn't jump off the back of the trash pile and I saw snakes everywhere I looked. With a gulp of air and a yell, I made two steps and landed in the field. I couldn't find anywhere that I had been bitten. And, as you can imagine, that was the last time I went exploring on the family's recycling ground.

My youngest uncle was only about ten years older than me. He was an important part of the farm labor until finishing High School and joining the military. He spent much time hunting and fishing with me when we could break from the farm work. One day he took me fishing on the Little Pee Dee River. We took my grandfather's boat and were in *hopes of bringing home some freshwater fish. We came to the river and launched into the water on a pleasant spring day. We took out our poles and worms and began searching the banks for fishing spots. As we began to fish, we began to find snakes. My uncle wasn't as afraid as I was. He was of course running the motor and controlling the boat. I was up front and along for the ride. That meant that I was the first to reach the overhanging limbs. It seemed that on that day most every limb was home to a snake. It was like that old song that talked about snakes hanging from the trees, "like sausage from the smokehouse wall." From one tree to another we saw snakes, snakes, and more snakes dangling and dropping from the limbs as we approached their resting place. I couldn't fish for watching and sliding opposite the snake infested limbs. My uncle just went on fishing and muttered, "Don't worry about the snakes, they won't hurt you." Fortunately, he was right that day. We never had one to fall into our boat or defend his limb from us. However, it was not an enjoyable day of fishing, at least for me.*

After finishing high school, I went to college and was only home for the summer. After entering seminary, I no longer returned home to work in the summer. I married my wife the summer of my college graduation and the next fall enrolled in seminary. My grandmother's health was starting to weaken noticeably and she was placed on more medications. The house in which she lived was built in the late fifties and was showing signs of aging like my grandmother. It was the fall of the year.

Everyone knows that in the fall of the year the mice began searching barns, buildings and houses for places to spend the winter. If they can find a small space around pipes or rotted boards, they will chew a hole just large enough to use as an entranceway into this warm residence and abundant supply of food. Unknown to my grandmother or my father, the mice had found a large enough space around pipes leading from the laundry room into the kitchen to make their way into Grandmother's home. It was soon evident that the mice were enjoying the kitchen too. So, Daddy began to take steps to remove the mice.

A rule of thumb is, "Where there are mice there are snakes!" Usually, snakes are seldom found in a home. Though mice squeeze in, snakes usually remain outside. This was not, however, a usual case. My mother and father came over daily and often several times each day to keep a check on my grandmother. Trouble, her faithful, but ugly four-legged companion, kept her company day and night. One day while checking on Grandmother she made the comment that she thought she saw a snake during the night. She wasn't sure if it was real or just a dream. Mom and dad passed it off as a side effect of the medications. After all Trouble was by her side and surely he would bark and alert her of the presence of a snake. She mentioned that she thought she had seen the snake on the mirror of her dresser. There seemed to be no evidence of a snake and so the event was passed off.

Sometime after Easter my grandmother's heart gave out. Mom and Dad were keeping a close eye on her because of the evident deterioration of her health. Mom and my oldest sister went over to see her and found her complaining of chest pain. Dad had gone to a doctor's appointment. They called the paramedics, but before they arrived, Grandmother passed through the temporal gates into the eternal world awaiting us. Mom was holding her in her arms.

After the funeral, the family returned to their normal lives. Daddy periodically walked through the empty house to be sure it was all right. While doing so he noticed something strange. It appeared to be bird droppings but there weren't any birds in the house. He then became suspicious that perhaps there really had been a snake after all. Several days later he entered the house at the right time. Down the hallway near the bathroom and my grandmother's bedroom a rather long chicken snake was lying on the floor. Daddy quickly looked for something with which to kill the snake, or contain it, and cornered the snake in the bathroom. He was able to remove it and rid the house of its unwanted occupant. He later found the enlarged hole that was big enough for mice and a snake to enter the house.

I have wondered what mysterious happenings took place during the night while Grandmother was still alive. I'm glad that ugly ol' Trouble was there to at least protect Grandmother from the snake getting into bed with her and giving her a heart attack prematurely.

Seven

Getting Ready for Winter

The mule barn where cows were fed for
butchering and hay was stored for the
winter feeding.

*The first sign of winter isn't the changing of
colors. It isn't the cooler nights and long
anticipated end to the tobacco gathering either.
No, the first sign of winter was the talk of school.
By mid-August the word "school" began creeping
back into our vocabulary. As Labor Day arrived
so did the beginning of school. Though I didn't
look forward to the return to desks, classrooms
and the daily regimen of mental exercising, I did
look forward to one event that always precipitated
our return to school, Treasure City. Treasure City
was a distant place that was larger than life and*

filled with most anything a dollar could buy. Every August, my family would crowd into the family car and make our way to Florence, a city about an hour's drive from my home. All summer, we children had worked on the farm. Unlike many others, my father, encouraged by governmental tax deductions and with my mother's prodding, I'm sure, paid his children for their work in gathering and preparing the tobacco for market. It was one of the first lessons in managing money and understanding the financial foundation for living. We were allowed to spend some of it on summer fun, but were cautioned to save the bulk of it for school supplies. School supplies included clothing. In today's language it would be considered one of those "win-win" situations. Daddy was respected for doing what few others were generous enough to do, and we returned the investment in greatly reducing the cost of sending us to school each year. On our part, we knew that working would bring us a financial benefit, and we could be more independent and "grown-up" by buying our own stuff.

As the table talk became more and more accustomed to chatter about returning to school, we began to make plans for our annual pilgrimage. The day would be set and the excitement would build. It was almost like Christmas. The difference was that we got to go through all the many items, and select the ones we wanted to take to, or wear to, school. And when we got to the checkout counter, we could pull out our wad of cash and amaze the clerk, as we paid our own way.

When the day finally arrived, we were up early and quickly gobbled down our breakfast, anxious to see the unbelievable warehouse of new things. The hour drive felt like an eternity. The trip was a marvelous journey beyond our small town and through places, hardly remembered, from the previous year. Across rivers, and through other small towns, past farms and workers in the fields we traveled, until we finally reached our destination. The parking lot was a huge field of asphalt. The big letters on the storefront, multitude of shopping carts and automatic opening front doors made the experience like walking into a dream world. The large aisles that made grocery stores look like a filling station went on and on. The long corridors of items, so wonderfully shiny and brand-new, brought shivers of delight to us kids off the farm. It was like walking through Santa's warehouse, except it was in the heat of August. But, the store was air-conditioned. We could run from aisle to aisle, and pick through the multitude of options, and never break a sweat.

After a while, we would settle down and begin the serious work of finding paper, notebooks, pencils, erasers, book sack, shoes, pants, shirts and whatever else we would need. Each child had their own shopping cart and soon it was time to checkout. With a little help from Mom and Dad, we unloaded the many supplies, and paid for each of them with our hard earned money. And with our exit to the car came the next great adventure, hamburgers. Not grilled in the backyard, or fried in the kitchen, but bought from a real hamburger place. It was a special treat to eat out and to enjoy the taste and atmosphere of a real hamburger restaurant. It was an added treat to an already wonderful day.

Once home again and settled into school, it was time for another custom of preparation. This was an annual custom for my father and me. My father would hook-up a flat bed trailer to the tractor and throw on an ax, the five horse David Bradley chainsaw with a bow blade, a wedge or two, some motor oil and gas, and we would head for the wooded area. It was time to cut wood for the winter.

Up until about high school age we heated with a wood heater. The heater was used during the winter months in the room connected to the kitchen and used as the gathering room. The other rooms in the house were left with what little heat circulated into them, which was very little. When spring returned the heater was removed giving us more room, which was always at a premium in a three bedroom house with five children and a mom and dad. Each fall Daddy would go to town and return with a heater, sometimes referred to as a trash burner. It was made of heavy tin and was only intended for the use of one year. The metal wasn't heavy enough to last very long in the intense heat but would, by spring, show signs of deterioration and breaking down. On many mornings, our little warm feet would be forced out from under the heavy covers and slammed down on the icy floors to transport our chilling bodies to the family room where we had heard Daddy starting the morning fire. We would arrive to the crackling and popping sound of the burning wood, and the familiar roar of the flames, and hot air rushing upward through the tin flue toward the chimney. Usually, the back of the thin walled heater was red-hot, as well as the tin flue at the heater and just above it. We would stand around the heater and rotate round and round trying to get both sides warm at the same time.

We would also, if coherent enough, bring our clothes for the day with us. Then, we could warm them and return to our rooms to put on warm clothing. Otherwise, our warm bodies quickly chilled as we returned to get ready for the day. If we still wanted to warm by the heater after dressing, we learned to be careful. It wasn't from being burned by the heater, however. After the early morning start-up, the intensity of the heat would be reduced, though you could still be burned very badly if you fell against the heater or touched it accidentally. The problem, however, was our clothing. We usually wore blue jeans. The heavy denim would warm up and hold the heat too well sometimes. Also, our blue jeans had those bronze pieces at various places, and when you started to move away from the heat, you found that the bronze heated faster and more intensely than the denim. As a result, you might wear an unseen, but sensitive red burn mark for a day or two.

So, in order to keep the family warm and reduce the cost of heat Daddy and I would make our way to the woods in search of a fallen tree, or some tree chosen for the sacrificial act. I just thank the Good Lord that I came up just in time to witness the chainsaw in action. The old crosscut saw hung on the barn wall. Daddy would tell stories of cutting wood, not many years earlier, with the crosscut saw as the only tool for cutting the tree into manageable blocks. For me it was simply to stay away from the falling tree and out of the way of the dangerous chain on the saw. I would help cut some of the small limbs with the ax and would mostly tote the blocks of wood as Daddy ran the chainsaw. Once we loaded them on the trailer, we unloaded them at home. Then it was time for the splitting. The wood needed to be split so they would fit into the heater and burn better. Some of the limbs could be left whole for burning. The sections from the tree's trunk and large limbs would need to be split. I never did much of the splitting. Even in early junior high school, I still couldn't hit the same cut twice or swing the ax with enough power to be very effective. I did find out that I could swing the ax hard enough to break *the handle. That may have been the biggest reason Daddy split the wood himself.*

Daddy enjoyed splitting the wood, I believe. It could be relaxing, though tiring for sure. We sometimes talked about it, and I often watched him do it with a grace and ease that left me to wonder why it was so difficult and unnatural for me. He knew the secret of how to split differing woods. Pine, for example, was soft and split more easily. I would watch him take a cut from the tree, but not split the section all the way across. Instead, he would, knowing the nature of the wood, work around the block, swinging the ax at an angle that popped off sticks of wood about the width of the ax and about two inches thick. It was an art that had been developed over many earlier years of practice. I also learned from him that oak, a very difficult wood to split, was saved until a hard freeze. On the morning following a hard freeze, he would arise early, and go to the woodpile while the ground and everything else was still frozen. He would take his ax and begin warming himself splitting the wood. When the wood was frozen it spit much easier than when thawed. I would sometimes awaken during winter to the sound of an ax splitting wood unaware that this was a sacrificial act of love.

Back in the fifties, sixties, and seventies, taking out the trash had a different meaning. Today we are dependent on trash pick-up or taking our refuse to recycle centers or disposal sites. In the middle of the 1900's, country folks had no trash pick-up. They also didn't have disposal sites or recycle centers to take their trash. This wasn't any big problem until the revolution of tin cans for canning and selling all sorts of food items, and the many metal containers and short-lived items for the house. The paper and wood items, or even furniture, would burn. However, the metal just got hot and slowly rusted. So most country dwellers, and for that matter, many of the town and city dwellers, had trash barrels, or a designated spot in the back yard where the trash was burned and reduced to the smallest amount possible.

We sometimes used a metal barrel that would quickly rust out due to the continual heat and damp outside conditions. My grandparents, who lived beside us, had their own barrel, and sooner or later a pile too. One of my jobs was the removing of the trash. This was usually a spring and fall job. After about six months of trash burning, you had a considerable pile of discarded metal and glass and other non-burnable items. I would get the tractor and trailer, and grab a six-pronged pitchfork, and set out to remove the metal and glass and leave the spot clean and ready for another six months of burning. I would pile the refuse on the trailer and then take it to the farm dumping ground at the back of the farm, excuse me, the farm-recycling center. It was a place where the land took a significant dip leaving *an area to throw the trash residue without creating a large pile. It was behind the tree line and a natural place for recycling. It was the place of the snake dens mentioned earlier.*

Once my cousin was helping me. As you can imagine, that had danger written all over it. We had a small trailer with sides and an open back. This would allow us to pile all the refuse on the trailer in one trip. I was standing on one side, and my cousin on the other, scooping with our pitchforks and forking the trash into the trailer. We were talking and laughing and making the best of the moment. I cannot recall the exact happenings, but remember well moving too far into the doorway of the trailer, for some unknown reason and feeling this jolt to my left arm. You guessed it. I had caught my cousin's pitchfork. The wound bled only a little bit and didn't hurt much, so we continued with our work, and I never mentioned it to my parents. It was one of those times when God was looking out for our ignorance. The wound never festered or gave me any problem. It healed, and left a little mark to remember the day by.

Another time, my sisters and I were playing around the burning trash pile. One of my sisters had put on a long discarded dress and was wearing it around the yard. In her playful wanderings, she came just a little too close to the burning pile, and suddenly the back of her dress was on fire. She naturally ran in fear of the fire.

We ran too, but we ran to stop her, and out the flames reaching up the back of her dress. Thankfully my mother saw the commotion and quickly ran out the house and caught my sister, and remembering to roll her on the ground in order to out fire on your clothing, put out the fire. She was okay and only frightened. After a few minutes we returned to our play.

One of our familiar patriotic hymns has the lyrics, "O beautiful for spacious skies, for amber waves of grain." There are times when a song is sung, a glimpse of the harvesting farmers at work or just some other little experience that occurs, and for a moment, I am back on a farm that was my childhood world. It was the place that taught me how to perceive life. It was the place that I discovered life, and established the values that still are firmly planted within me. But at those moments, it is a place that I loved more than I knew, and a place that gives me identity. I still have the privilege today to walk the fields of my father's farm. Many of the familiar landmarks have disappeared. Yet, with every walk comes a flood of memories and a special warmth within. It is said that a farmer has to be born with a love for the land. No other power is strong enough to enable him to endure the struggles, heartaches and sacrifices needed to work the soil. I have never regretted my calling to serve as a minister. I have never wished to go back and plot another course. But still today, as I walk the fields of my childhood and youth, there comes from within a recognition that this isn't just land, it is me. The barns, the fields, the trees and the old hand pump way off in the field is who I am. I am, and always will be, a boy from the farm, nothing great or special, just an ordinary soul mysteriously connected with a small plot of farm dirt.

On the farm, there is something special about the fall. It is more than a time of beautiful colors and enjoyable holiday celebrations. It's a time of harvest like the familiar scene of the Pilgrims and Indians eating together. The hymns, that say thanks to God for his bounty, are for the farmers a life experience. They tended the grain and watched it grow. They know their dependence upon the uncontrollable things in life that have to work in their favor. They see daily that all our work and wisdom cannot make seeds sprout or plants grow. They live closest to God's daily work in nature. It is on the farm that the harvest is truly not something we did or earned but God's gift and we are simply gleaning from His garden.

With the end of the hard work of tobacco season and the entrance back into school comes the fall. By October, the harvest season is ready. The real money was in tobacco. No other crop could produce the cash needed to support a family, other than tobacco. And the reality was that tobacco was becoming less and less able to do so. Each farmer was struggling with how much to expand in hopes of continuing farming, and when it was time to get out of the business. So, the harvest season was a time of traditional farming that served two main purposes. First, it provided food materials for the livestock. It was food for horses, mules, cows, hogs, chickens and whatever else might eat corn. They were glad to see the fall harvest coming in. Corn was an essential, and up until the sixties, was still gathered by hand. I can remember, as a small child, going with my father and others into the rows of corn, and seeing them break off the ears, and pile them together in what was called a heap row. Several rows were broken at the time, and the piles were left in one row, to later be thrown onto a drag pulled by a mule, or later a trailer pulled by a tractor.

The corn was then taken to the corncrib, a place where the corn was stored, usually in the mule barn or near the animals. Now that the corn was protected from the weather, the farmer could, on rainy days, and at other times when free to do so, strip the ears of the shucks, and grind off the kernels of corn on the hand turned corn sheller. For many, the hand turned corn sheller wasn't available, and they would develop calluses and raw spots on their hands shelling the corn from its cob. Once shelled, the corn was fed to the animals.

However, corn wasn't just for the animals. We farmers enjoyed it too. One of the South's familiar foods is grits. I've discovered, in reading about the early settlement of America, the essential nature of corn. It was, without a doubt, the one *food that enabled the English settlers to survive. For southern farm families it wasn't that essential, but it was an important part of our diet too. Whether grits, cornmeal, corn on the cob or corn creamed or fried it was still a staple. Field corn was not as good as sweet corn for cooking, or boiling on the cob. But, it was often used when the sweet corn was not available.*

Another staple to many farmers was "corn squeezings." It is better known as "white light'ning" or "moonshine." It was a common alcoholic beverage that was made from corn, along with other untold additives. The story was often told in my childhood how my grandfather and a couple of his brothers tried to rid Columbus County, a connecting county with Horry County in neighboring North Carolina, of moonshine. The story goes that my grandfather tried to find and destroy all the liquor stills possible. He worked for the Tobacco, Tax and Alcohol Commission doing just that. As for his brothers, they tried to drink every drop of the stuff they could find. The availability and low cost of alcohol did away with most of the stills. I can remember running across some white light'ning during my high school years, and seeing my friend pour some of it out, and ignite it with a match. It was still being made in the Seventies by a secretive few.

As combines came on the scene, the hand breaking of the ears and shucking and shelling of the corn faded away. the growing of soybeans, wheat and other crops was increased with the advent of the combine harvester. Few farmers farmed enough land or had enough financial strength to purchase a combine. However, one or two would go out on a financial limb to purchase one, in the hopes that others would hire him to gather their corn, wheat, oats or soybeans. The differing crops didn't require a different combine, but just a different head that gathered the crop into the mouth of the combine. Corn required one kind of head, and soybeans, oats and wheat all shared a different head. They use the familiar head with the large turning paddle wheel to brush the grain stalks to the cutters and into the combine's inner machinery. Some farmers found the large investment a good one as they stayed busy late into the night, gathering the harvest for friends, and making a little extra cash too.

Other crops were planted, but were basically an extra cash crop. Soybeans and wheat were sometimes planted, but they were planted on land not being used for tobacco and corn, or after corn was harvested as a late fall or winter crop. They were also a crop that the farmer hoped would bring in some extra cash, though usually not much, to help with the many expenses.

Another crop, often planted in the late fall and at various other times during the year, was oats. Oats were usually a cover crop. They were used to cover the soil until time to prepare it for planting more essential crops. Oats were sometimes used for a supplement in cattle and horse feed. We usually used them for grazing the cattle in late fall and early spring. Oats are a hearty crop that can take the cold weather and continue growing. They are therefore a good crop to plant, and let the cows graze, to reduce the need for hay. Sometimes the oats were actually harvested. I remember several times bailing the stalks for hay. The cows didn't really like them but they would do in a pinch. The cows preferred harvesting them green and over a long period of time.

By Thanksgiving, the harvest was usually in, and the fields were a golden glow of stubbles and discarded stalks. This would be turned under to rot and provide nutrients for future corps, unless a quick planting was planned. If that was the case, the stubbles and stalks were burned and then the field was disked so a new crop could be planted more quickly. As the days continued to grow shorter, and the temperatures colder, another fall occasion arrived, hog killing.

Hog killing required a lengthy spell of cold weather. If the meat was to be preserved, unless you were fortunate enough to own a new freezer, you were dependent upon cold enough weather to keep the meat from spoiling until it was salted and cured properly. So the farmer who wanted to kill a hog fattened for just the occasion watched for the winter winds to blow in days and nights that kept the temperatures below forty and would give sufficient time for curing the meat.

Hog killing was a long day's work. It began with the building of a large fire and the sharpening of knives. The fire would burn all day, but for different purposes. First, was the boiling of water. A large vat, or metal barrel, was used to boil water for scalding the hog. The first thing was to shoot the hog. That was not so simple. A hog's brain isn't that large, even though his head is, and knowing where to put the bullet is important. I have heard many stories of how the marksman missed his mark, and the hog would literally spit out the bullet. Other stories are told of how the hog was shot and had a bullet lodged somewhere in his snout, but was virtually unhurt by the event. He, then of course, ran off, aware that the farmer wasn't just feeding him, and now the element of surprise was gone. What was left was a tricky game of chess in which the farmer tried to corner the hog for another shot. Once accomplished, the bulky and weighty carcass had to be taken to the waiting boiling water. This was accomplished by pulling the dead animal. The real tricky part was lifting this animal, and lowering him into the scalding water without getting scalded in the process.

The scalding process was as essential for hogs as it was for chickens. Killing chickens always required you to do the same procedure on a smaller scale. The chicken was placed into boiling water for just a minute, and once pulled out the earlier difficulty of removing the feathers was made much easier. Hogs are hairy animals. To remove the hair, since the skin would be eaten as well, was important. So into the boiling water the hog would go, and carefully the water would be poured over his entire body until ready for cleaning. Now, the hair could be pulled and scraped until the skin was clean, and free of hair. Now came the gruesome work.

The hog was hung by his back legs with his head just off the ground. An incision was begun between the back legs and was cut down to the chest cavity. This allowed for the removal of the much desired inner organs. Chitterlings, the intestines (pronounced chitlins), were to be washed and later eaten or used as casing for the sausage. The stomach, liver, heart and other unidentified delicacies were to be carefully protected for future consumption. It was often said that the only part of a pig that wasn't eaten was his squeal. That was more true than I ever liked. Hogshead cheese, hog brains in scrambled eggs, pigs feet and liver pudding or liver and rice were not on my menu of enjoyable foods.

While the internal organs were removed, the water was replaced by a large cast iron pot for cooking cracklings. Into the kettle was thrown strips and chunks of fat. The fatty tissue cooked down leaving little crunchy chunks and a liquid known as lard. The chunks were removed from the lard and became an enjoyable first treat for the workers.

Each family, or community, had its designated butcher. This person would lead in the cutting of the animal into parts separating the loins from the bacon, the ham from the hocks and the various meat cuts that would lead to a winter of enjoyable pork consumption. It was usually a busy day, and a day filled with laughter and family time together.

Once cut, the meat was taken to the smokehouse. Behind my grandmother's house the old smokehouse stood for many years. It was used for storage but still had the enjoyable smell associated with it. Many times, the smokehouse was hung with meat, rubbed in salt and seasoning in smoke, for a winter meal. Sausage, ham, shoulders, bacon, fatback and more all hung and waited its day on the table.

Once the meat was all separated, the chitterlings washed, brains removed and cracklings cooked attention was turned to sausage. Sausage was where all the unknown and small pieces of meat and fat were put. The meat was cut fine, or ground, and then spiced up. It was then placed into a press that would force the sausage into its casing. It was then hung in the smokehouse for preserving. The dawn of refrigerators and freezers made easier work of preparing the meat as they replaced the smokehouse. However, the smokehouse flavor was never duplicated.

With the long day of hog killing over, the way was prepared for a long winter and a festive celebration of Christmas.

Eight

My Uncle's Flying Machine

One of my father's brothers had moved away long
before I had developed a memory. My first
memories of him were of a slender and energetic
man, partially bald and having only one eye. He
and one of his brothers were fighting over a
pocketknife in their childhood years and when the
wrestling match ended, he had an eye wound.
When taken to the doctor, the doctor sadly
reported that if the knife blade had been a fraction
of an inch other than where it was, the eye could
have been saved. Instead, the eye would have to be

removed. I seldom remember him wearing a patch, but usually a pair of glasses with the lens of the missing eye frosted. He was a man of determination, so a minor handicap wasn't going to be a hindrance for him.

In my first memories he lived in Chicago. He was married, and he and his wife had two girls. When they would come down on vacation they would stay at my grandmother's, and that was, of course, only about seventy-five yards from my house. We, therefore, had lots of time to talk and become reacquainted with our northern cousins. Being Southerners, we thought their pronunciations were funny. Being raised in Chicago, they thought the same about us. It was an interesting time of getting reacquainted each summer, and rediscovering a way of communication so different than ours.

I didn't know much about my uncle's occupation in Chicago. I knew that he was a mechanical person and pretty quick to figure out problems and solutions. He was good working with his hands. He did much for my grandmother while down on vacation each year.

I, first, began to know him, as he and several of his brothers would setup a table out under the pecan trees and break out the cards. They would sit under one of the trees and play cards for hours. I would often sit with them, and listen to the conversations, and try to figure out what

*manner of cards they were playing. I never got it.
It was called pinochle. It required a special deck,
and I could never figure out why most all the
number cards were missing. Nonetheless, they
would laugh, talk, poke fun at each other and be
brothers sharing a moment of passing time
together.*

*About junior high age, I heard that my uncle was
moving back home. They would move back to our
town and find work to make ends meet. They
returned, and found a house in town, and soon
blended into the flow of our community. Being
gone for many years, and being out of the local
culture, led them to adopt ways that seemed
foreign to us at times. No big issues or major
problems, just a puzzled question of why they
didn't did things like we always do them. My
uncle, and his wife, who came from Kentucky, had
moved to the Windy City and found a freedom to
rediscover their way of life. Gone were the family
and community expectations and pressures to live
and think a certain way. They were free to make
their own choices, and the community around
them offered many differing ways to live than the
small southern community of his, or her,
childhood. When they returned to the South to live
within my community, their freedom stood out
among the long held Southern traditions. It was
my first look across the fence of Southern social
expectations. It was also a place for me to begin
evaluating what I would personally accept and*

reject, as I was now on the verge of the volatile adolescent years.

At first, I only knew my uncle as he came to the farm regularly. I would get to help him and talk with him. Somehow, I developed a close connection with him. Maybe, it was just two hardheaded and determined persons who could work together. Maybe, it was just being enamored with a relative that had been outside of our normal world, and had returned with many different ideas and ways that I wanted to explore. He had learned many tricks for using his hands to create things. Being mechanically minded, and enjoying working with my hands too, we naturally hit it off together well. Whether working together on a building project on the farm, or one of the many craft projects at his workshop, I enjoyed the opportunity to learn and observe his skills.

Those skills fed into his one passion, to fly. Somewhere, beyond the bounds of his childhood farm, he had seen and determined to join those who flew for the love of flying. When he returned to my hometown, he had already purchased the plans for making an airplane, and dreamed of flying it one day. When I received my driver's license, I would regularly stop to talk with him, and help him work on his dream. He was using wood, and had to cut the pieces exactly according to the plans. He had to use epoxy glue to seal the many pieces together. He would spend hour after hour working on the complicated inner supports for the large wing. It was a long and slow process. He didn't have a lot of time to work on it. However, it was one of those passions that, when a minute was had, it was spent on the long-cherished dream. For several years he worked on it on weekends and afternoons. And slowly, ever so slowly, the pieces began to resemble parts of an airplane.

One afternoon, as I stopped to talk and watch him work, he told me that he was buying an airplane. I was amazed. He told me it was a homemade aircraft much like the one he was making. Since his was taking so long, he had decided to buy the airplane and rebuild it. I was excited of course and could hardly wait to see it. It was located at a private airstrip near Chadbourn, North Carolina, about thirty minutes away. We would need to go to the airstrip and remove the propeller and wing, so as to transport the plane on a trailer to my uncle's yard.

The day finally arrived and we, and several others, made the trip and got our first sight of the yellow homemade aircraft. It was a tail dragger with a small wheel to protect the tail from the ground. The seat on which the pilot and one passenger could ride was the centerpiece of the wing. You had to carefully step beside the cockpit so as not to damage the cloth covered wing that was hollow except for the inner supports. All this would be stripped away, and the inner wooden pieces inspected and repaired, and then recovered.

We began the process of unbolting the wing from the fuselage and removing the landing gear so the plane could be placed on the trailer and carted to its new home. We made it back to Loris without incident, and put the plane under my uncle's garage for protection.

Over the next many months, I would spend my spare time by my uncle's side, as he worked on this plane, with a renewed passion to fly looking down on the earth. He stripped the covering from the wing and replaced the broken, rotted or damaged inner supports. He then worked on the fuselage to do the same. There was no major damage, just a broken piece here and there, and a place or two where water had seeped in and deteriorated the wood. Everything had to be just right. After all, it would be no fun to see your ride coming apart several hundred feet off the ground. The plane was listed as an Experimental Aircraft. That meant that it was in a special class of handmade aircraft that had certain regulations, but was given much freer restrictions than factory-built aircraft. There were several men in our area that were members of the Experimental Aircraft Association, and met to talk and share ideas and their love of flying.

With the wing and fuselage repairs now completed it could be covered once more. This was a technical and tedious task of mixing material and solvents to create a flexible, but firm shell over the wing and fuselage. It took hours to get the material over the parts and then to treat it so the pressure of flying, and the sun and rain would not break the protective skin of the aircraft.

With the body of the plane ready, it was time to work on the cockpit and engine. The instruments were all cleaned and checked for accuracy. The instrument panel was refinished and readied for the instruments. The plexiglas was replaced in the doors and windshield. Then the motor was cleaned and double-checked. The motor was to be rebuilt after a certain number of hours used. The propeller was sent off to be refinished and checked for proper blade slope. With all this completed, it was then time to reassemble the plane.

First, came the mounting of the wing and the landing gear to the fuselage. Then, came the mounting of the motor and instruments. Then, came the finishing touches of the cockpit. And, with that the plane was ready for testing. But, how do you test a plane in the middle of a small-town neighborhood? Simple, you tie its tail to a substantial tree and fire up the engine. I was amazed as my uncle simply tied the tail of the plane to a pine tree in his yard and fired up the motor with the propeller whirling. I am not sure what the neighbors thought, but I'm sure they were glad when it was time to take it to the airport several miles away.

For many days, my uncle would check cables and make minor adjustments. Then, he would climb into the cockpit and fire the engine. The propeller *would whirl around making the familiar and unmistakable sound of an object cutting through the air. Then he would start to ease back on the throttle. The engine would roar a higher pitch and the propeller would increase the sound of slicing and pushing the air. And then, as the throttle was pulled back a little more, it happened. No, the plane didn't break loose from the tree and take off down the street. The plane's landing gear slowly rose off the ground. At that moment we knew the motor and propelling mechanism was sufficient to send the plane airborne. It was always a thrill to hear the motor roar and see the two tires attached to the wing lift off the ground.*

Finally, the day came. My uncle viewed Sunday as a day to accomplish the many things that didn't get done throughout the week. He knew that Sunday was one of the least traveled days for the small-town streets and roads. Therefore, he asked me to help him transport the plane to the airport on a Sunday morning. This was one of those things that was uncustomary for my family and community. Being a teenager with my own natural tendencies to cross the customary lines, I accepted his offer, and agreed to meet him early one Sunday morning.

I arose early and drove my pickup, which would be needed for the effort, to my uncle's house. We connected the plane to the pickup by placing its tail on the back and attaching it to the truck. The plane's wing was short enough that the plane could be pulled down the streets and major roads without being hindered by the signs on the side of the road. It was a slow and persistent journey to the airport. The airport was located about two miles north of town. It took a while, but we made it before the church traffic hit the highway.

Once at the airport, we spent the rest of the morning testing the plane by taxiing up and down the airstrip testing and retesting the controls. It was an exciting day that would end in disappointment.

The testing process was to get a good feel for the aircraft, and to build up confidence, before committing your well being to the aircraft completely. So up and down, down and up, up and down he went. He would wind-up the motor and go down the runway, slowly increasing the speed and feeling for the plane's response. The plane was light and designed to fly at fairly slow speeds. For that reason, my uncle had to be careful to get almost enough speed to take off, but not too much and take off prematurely. That was where the disappointment came in.

As I watched the taxiing, I could feel the anticipation building. Unnoticed by us was a gentle breeze that sprang up. Up and down the runway the plane taxied, faster and faster it went. And then a little hop, and the plane was airborne for just a moment, and then off the throttle, and back down on the runway. That was a critical speed. At the moment the plane leaves *the earth the steering mechanism for taxiing is no longer useful. Instead, the plane is totally dependent upon the rear movable wing and tail parts to guide the plane by the wind flow. At that moment of lifting off and quickly returning, there was a moment when the plane was basically uncontrollable. That is the moment of decision. Either the pilot pushes the plane past it by full throttle and takes off, or the pilot tries to avoid it by staying on the ground. With no wind, the plane can flirt with danger, and pop up and drop down regaining control with the ground steering system.*

As my uncle tempted fate by a brief lift off, without the intentions of flying off, a gust of wind caught the plane, and as he came back down on the runway, the plane took a sudden turn to the right and moved through the grassy area toward the ditch bordering the highway beside the runway. The landing gear stopped in the ditch and the plane finally sat still. My uncle had tried to brake and regain control, but being in that no man's land left him helpless to control the plane. All he could do was to try to slow it and hope for as little damage as possible. The damage was only slight, but the propeller caught most of it and would need to be sent off and made straight again. That would take several weeks, and until done the plane was left to sit among the other planes waiting for someone to bring them to life.

As the minor repairs were being completed, two events occurred that kept me from ever flying with my uncle in the familiar yellow experimental aircraft. First was an opportunity to purchase a Cherokee 150 that a friend of his had. The second was an offer to purchase the plane he had worked so hard on for so long. He sold the yellow plane and made arrangements to purchase the Cherokee.

It was the joy of his life to say the least. On a number of occasions, I was able to go with my uncle up for a ride around the county. We would fly to Conway and visit the airport there. We would fly up through the fluffy clouds and see the earth from the bird's eye view, literally. Once we were flying and he was explaining to me the homing device used to guide you on long distance trips. He showed me how to set the radio on a certain frequency for a specific homing transmitter and to follow the signal until needing to switch to another. He said, "Hey I'll show you one if you want." I of course said, "yes," and we set the radio for a signal transmitted just outside of Florence, South Carolina. We followed the signal for the fifty miles to Florence and then he made a circular sweep and said, "look down there." There, just off the Pee Dee shortcut from Highway 301 and 76 to I 95, which came a few years later, was a large object that looked similar to a bowling pin. It stood in the middle of a field, and was surrounded by a chain-linked fence. We returned to Loris and landed safely. From time to time, we continued to enjoy a flight together and enjoy the special feeling of looking down on the earth.

As I finished my High School years, I became more and more busy courting, and less and less involved flying with my uncle. I eventually went to college, and it was while I was in college that I received a message at breakfast that I needed to call home. I called home and Mom told me the news that my uncle's plane had crashed near Charleston on a flight back from Georgia. His wife was with him, and they had become caught in an approaching storm, rushing to return home. When I arrived home later that day, my father and an older brother had gone to make a positive identification. They later arrived back home and as my father saw me waiting, we simply embraced and wept. I had lost an uncle that had taught me much, and allowed me to visit with him in his dream world. Dad had lost a younger brother and a part of his family world. The funeral and days surrounding it are still a blur. My grandmother later wrote about the incident.

"In this sad world of ours, sorrow comes to all and it often comes with bitter agony. Perfect relief is not possible except with time. You cannot now believe that you will ever feel better, but this is not true, you are sure to be happy again. Knowing this and truly believing it will make you less miserable now.

Read in God's Word 1 Thessalonians 5:17-18, "Pray constantly, give thanks in all circumstances; for this is the will of God in Christ Jesus for you." NIV

Read 1 Peter 5:7, "Cast all your anxieties on him, for He cares about you." NIV

After Richard and Margaret were killed so suddenly, I felt like I could not stand it, but these verses helped me so much. I've never gotten over it but God has a purpose in everything and we learn to accept it."

On many occasions I travel the Pee Dee shortcut road. Always, I look for the homing transmitter and remember the day I viewed it from the air with my uncle in his flying machine.

Aunt Margaret, Uncle Richard and
Lynn

Nine

A Heritage Worth Keeping

This chapter is intended to relay a trail of honored and respectful living. I will here tell the story of my family heritage for my children and the relatives of John Edward Prince in particular. As each family has two streams of heritage, I will also bring out the heritage of Isaac Jackson Spivey. If you are reading this and not part of the John Edward Prince and Isaac Jackson Spivey family, forgive me for this specific focus. I hope in reading this you will be able to remember some of your heritage and be a better person in your family line who lives honorably and respectfully.

Photo made c1875

His name was John Edward Prince. He married Mary Price and thus began his family. His heritage can be traced back to the late 1600's in America. His great, great grandfather, Nicholas Prince, born in 1738, lived in Virginia but moved into the southeastern part of North Carolina. While in North Carolina his wife gave birth to a son, Nicholas R. Prince, in 1758. When his son was three years old Nicholas, the father, and his family moved near Marion, South Carolina. In 1761, Nicholas Prince moved from Marion District to settle in The Independent Republic of Horry County. He moved into the area of Horry County known as Kingston Parish. There he raised his family.

Nicholas R. Prince was about 35 when the Revolutionary War began. He enlisted with the Fourth Regiment of the South Carolina Continental Line and was eventually assigned to Charleston. He worked there making ammunition for the artillery. When Charleston was captured by British forces, Nicholas R Prince was among those captured. Though I do not know how it occurred, it is recorded that he, along with others, eluded their British captors and fled back to Horry County. There he once more volunteered to stand with Peter Horry and General Francis Marion for the Patriot's cause. He survived the war and you can research more information about his service and involvements.

Nicholas Prince returned back to Horry County to live with his wife. They had a son in 1784 and named him Nicholas R. Prince Jr. I know little about Nicholas Jr. other than he too lived on the family plantation in the Kingston Parish section of Horry County. In 1828 he had a son and named him Lott Prince.

Lott had four children by his first wife, Celia Ann Hardee and one by his second wife, Irena Bryant. One of the first four children was a son, John Edward Prince. Following the birth of his last child, and the infant's death, Lott volunteered to serve in the Confederate Army. He served in the 10th Regiment Company C, of the Confederate Army. I do not know the details, but in 1864 while in service and stationed in Knoxville Tennessee, Lott Prince died, or was killed, while in the uniform of the Confederacy.

Lott's son, John Edward Prince, was born in 1850. He was just fourteen when he received the news of his father's death. John Prince was crippled from birth. It is said that his siblings placed him in a wheelbarrow and carried him to school as a child. He was able to gain some use of his legs, but lived with a crippled left hand. I have one picture of him on a tin plate that dates back to around the 1870's. In it you can see his left hand *held to his chest and obviously distorted from its normal size.*

I have yet to get information on why and when, but John Edward Prince moved to Loris, in Horry County, where he settled and raised a large family. He and his wife, Mary Price, had nine children. They lived in a large two-story house that sat on the southwest corner of Highway 701 and Main Street. John and Mary turned their home into a boarding house. Many of the tobacco buyers stayed there during the buying season as well as many other guests throughout the year. John Prince served as a school teacher. I have no records of his years of service or place of teaching other than he began at the age of nineteen and taught in the Horry County school District.

At an unknown time, he became the Justice of the Peace for Loris. Records from 1915 show him as the "Trial Justice" for Loris. My grandmother, his daughter, told me on several occasions one particular memory she had of helping him. As Justice of the Peace, he had the authority to perform the marriage ceremony for those choosing him to do so. From time to time a couple would knock on the door of the boarding house and ask for the justice, or magistrate as my grandmother would say, to marry them. It usually occurred in the evening hours, when the day's work was over. On several occasions, when this would take place, my grandmother would run stand beside her father as he talked with the couple. He would then look over to his daughter and say, "Retha will you help me carry the lantern to the office so I can marry this couple." She, of course, eagerly ran for the lantern, and they would walk down Main Street together until reaching his office, she providing the hand to replace her father's crippled hand.

Records show that John Edward Prince was in Loris when town officials petitioned the state to recognize Loris as a municipality in 1902. When the petition was filed to make Loris a city of Horry County, South Carolina, John Edward Prince was one of the names listed on the petition. He is said to have had several businesses, one of which was the boarding house. It was one of the first businesses to start in Loris. Though I do not know when he started as the "Trial Justice" for Loris, records from 1915 show he was serving in that office then.

John Edward Prince died in 1916 at the age of 66. My grandmother was only thirteen when her father passed away. She helped her mother with the boarding house until age sixteen when a tall, confident and handsome man won her heart. However, like the rest of her siblings, her father left her with a farm of about 60 acres as his gift of love. She married and left home one month short of her 17th birthday.

The other stream flows from Isaac Jackson Spivey.

Victor Grantham Spivey, his son, had a heritage of his own. His ancestry can be traced all the way back to England. Isaac Jackson Spivey and his forefathers has long settled in Columbus County, North Carolina. Most were from an area known as Iron Hill, which is located just east of Tabor City. My grandfather's grandfather was Caleb

Photo date unknown.

Spivey. He too served in the Confederate Army. He returned home after the war and lived till 1892. The home in which he lived still stands in Iron Hill and is still inhabited. Several years ago, I developed a friendship with a couple who bought an old house from the 1800's and were restoring it. I learned that their house was the Caleb Spivey house. They invited me to come see it sometime and I was greatly excited to do so. They worked hard to keep the house as it was in the 1800's. They even had a picture of Caleb and his son on the wall of an upstairs room of the two-story house.

As best as I remember, Caleb was in the artillery unit during the Civil War. As a result, his hearing was so damaged that he was barely able to hear.

In 1865, he had a son, Isaac Jackson Spivey. He, too remained in Tabor City and was known to be a very good carpenter. I have the wooden carpenter's box in which he stored his tools. I also have several carpentry tools which belonged to Isaac, my great grandfather Spivey.

In 1899, Isaac Spivey had a son named Victor Grantham Spivey. Granddaddy, as I shall refer to him, was a tall, confident and straight-up-the-lime man. He was very athletic in school, and is said to have been scouted by several colleges for their athletic programs. He was fast on his feet. The outbreak of World War I changed any athletic interests which he may have had.

He had a farm in the Tabor City area where he and Grandmother lived. I have seen the picture of him in his World War I uniform. I understand that his involvements in service were minimal as he was inducted just in time for the war to be over. When Grandaddy returned from the service, he chose to work with the North Carolina Police. He eventually transferred from being a police officer to working with the Tobacco, Tax and Alcohol Commission. He focused on finding and destroying liquor stills. It is said that he, and several of his brothers, tried to remove all the liquor from Columbus County. Granddaddy would search for the stills and destroy them while his brothers drank all they could get. Granddaddy was a live-by-the-book and suffer-the-weight-of-the-law man. He worked in various parts of Columbus County. He was greatly irritated and angered whenever he took the owner of a liquor still before a judge that, due to relationships or organizational ties, would set the law-breaker free with little or no punishment.

My father, from time to time, would help my grandfather when searching for a still. Granddaddy gave my father a pistol and told him, if need be, use it without hesitation. The usual part for my father was to drive the car for my grandfather. A major eruption occurred once when my grandfather's car was found burnt with his handcuffs hanging on the steering wheel. Things quieted down, for all but the moonshiners, when my grandfather was located and everyone realized my grandfather was still alive.

Daddy told me that Granddaddy, and usually one other person, would have Daddy drop them off at a designated place. Granddaddy would tell my father, "Earl, you be back at," a designated time, "and look for us. If you do not see us do not stop or wait. Keep moving." Granddaddy was always there for a quick jump into the car and ride back home.

Partly due to frustration with the connections that hindered the prosecuting of moonshiners in Columbus County and also the opportunity to serve more effectively elsewhere, Granddaddy accepted an assignment to serve in Virginia.

My grandfather had a sharp sense of direction. When working in Virginia, he would fly over a specific area looking for the early morning column of smoke rising from a liquor still. It is said that he could get his bearings, drive to a nearby location, and walk straight to the still. It wasn't until I was a youth and watched the movie, "Walking Tall," that I got a good look at my grandfather's work.

I remember staying with my grandfather while my mother took my grandmother shopping. He had, what was then known as hardening of the arteries, dementia and was reliving his past. I watched one day as he shuffled into the sitting room where I was. "They are out there. Can you see them over there?" As he came to the door going into the kitchen, he put one hand on the doorpost and picked up one foot, as if stepping over something, and then the next foot. I was confused over what he was doing until I saw the movie. I then learned that a routine warning device for the moonshiners was to run a wire around the still at a distance that would provide them with a good warning that someone outside their group was approaching. The wire would be attached to something that would make a loud noise if the wire was hit by someone walking.

I remember as a child seeing the copper tubing and other items taken from a still, as well as dynamite and the caps to ignite them. When a still was taken, what the law wanted was taken and the rest was blown to smithereens, as we say.

Granddaddy's career was cut short as he retired at an early age. His retirement was more forced than chosen. While on duty in Virginia, he and his partner were approaching a house near where they had found a liquor still. Before reaching the door, a shotgun blast came from inside blowing a hole through the chest of his partner. I do not recall any description of what took place afterwards. The one who shot Granddaddy's partner was arrested and stood trial. He was found guilty and sentenced to many years of imprisonment.

But to Granddaddy's great anger a judge relieved the man from his sentence for personal reasons and released him from prison. That was much the same as waving a matador's cape before an angry bull. Granddaddy's live-by-the-law principle would not allow him to stand by and just let go of such an injustice. So up the judicial ladder Granddaddy went, demanding a correction to the injustice. His superiors finally told him, "Victor, either let it go or we will have to transfer you to South Carolina." Partly, due to his devotion to his partner, and because of his refusal to accept anything less than the law, Granddaddy was transferred to Florence, South Carolina, about 50 miles from Loris. He shortly took their offer of retirement and came home to his wife and family.

In 1905, John Edward Prince purchased a farm of about 60 acres from Wilson Manasseh Suggs. The farm was one mile south of Main Street,

Loris. He gave it to his daughter, Retha Prince Spivey, wife of

Victor Spivey. Dad said that he was in early elementary school when they moved from the farm in Tabor, Granddaddy's farm, to this one in Loris. With Daddy being born in 1924, that would have to be sometime about 1930. The 1920 U. S. Census records show Victor and Retha Spivey living in Tabor City. The 1930 census records show them living in the Simpson Creek District just outside of Loris. Most of Granddaddy and Grandmother's children would have grown up here in Loris on the old home site. A new home was built in the late 1950's. I do remember Daddy riding with me over to Tabor City one day when his memory was still accurate. He told me to go down a certain street and he would show me the house in which he was born. I slowed down, and he pointed out a white wooden house, with a porch and a well in the back yard. "There is where I was born" he said. As of 2022 the house is still standing. Having the opportunity to serve as the supply pastor for Tabor City Baptist Church, I, from time to time, drive slowly by the house and look to see if Daddy and his brothers might be playing in the yard.

With Granddaddy spending weeks at a time in Virginia, Grandmother was busy with raising a family of six boys, the seventh was to come a few

years later, and the much work to be done on the farm. Grandmother was an excellent cook. She helped her mother with the cooking for the boarding house. She was always busy either in the garden or the kitchen. As her sons graduated from high school, they were quick to leave the farm for more education, or to explore and conquer their part of the world. Most spent time in the military. Two were medically discharged due to injuries suffered in service. Three served differing times, with one of them retiring from the military. Two never served. One uncle was not allowed to serve, due to losing an eye in an accident as a child. My father was the other. He ran a dairy immediately after graduation. It was considered an essential business for the community, and his being drafted was deferred. When his deferment was up, he went to enlist, but World War II had just ended, and he was free to return home.

Spivey's Meadowlawn Dairy was a joint partnership between my father and his father. Granddaddy financed the operation and Daddy ran the business. For about ten years my father ran the dairy with the help of my grandmother and his younger brothers. He started while still in school with a few cows and a bicycle for deliveries. He started the business with a horse and buggy delivering the milk. Partly, due to demand and perhaps more due to a mishap, Daddy purchased a truck for the daily deliveries to people in Loris.

The mishap occurred one morning when making the routine milk deliveries. As Daddy, or one of his brothers, would take the horse into town, they would stop at the homes purchasing milk, both plain and chocolate. I didn't know chocolate was offered, until finding caps for the milk bottles, that were for chocolate milk. This day would leave a lasting memory. While removing the milk from the buggy, and placing it on the door step of one of the homes, something spooked the usually docile horse. With a sudden burst of fear, and a determination to find safety, the horse burst into a gallop, disregarding the buggy and milk in tow, not to mention the shouting of the one making the deliveries. All might have been fine, except the horse came to a brick wall, that it was able to clear, but the buggy didn't. When the horse was retrieved, there were only remnants of what used to be a wooden buggy in tow.

Daddy had actually begun the dairy while he was in school, which only went to the eleven grade back then. He liked cows and until his declining years always had a small herd on the farm.

Grandmother would churn butter that was sold along with the milk. It is more likely that her sons were kept busy by doing the work of churning. I do remember seeing an electric churn she had, though I never saw her use it. She would just give me a large glass jar with raw milk and say, "Shake it till it turns to butter." I usually had to stop for a break or two, but eventually, the white liquid turned into a yellowish solid, that was put into a mold, until it was firm. One of my sisters still has a couple of the wooden molds.

With Daddy's brothers all gone, except the youngest, continuing the dairy became more consuming. I remember Daddy telling me of the difficulty he had staying awake in church on Sunday mornings. Daddy would awake well before sunrise to gather the cows into the milk barn. They went to their usual stall where their head was secured enabling them to eat the feed that lured them to the twice a day ritual. While they ate Daddy would attach a vacuum milking system to their udders. When he began the dairy, he milked each cow by hand. But he soon purchased the vacuum driven system that greatly increased the productivity of the dairy. Even after the dairy was closed, Grandmother kept a milk cow or two for getting fresh milk. Either she or Daddy would milk them by hand. I have several memories of being with both of them as they milked the cows. I, however, never learned the skill. I just watched and toted the bucket of milk.

By the time the cows were milked, the milk filtered and bottled, the bottles delivered and Daddy had returned home, it was close to church time. With a quick clean-up, Daddy would join my mom and oldest sister for the ride to church. As he sat listening to the sermon, the weight of a day's work left him struggling with the heaviness of sleep. He often lost the battle, drifting off for a few minutes of rest. He once apologized to the pastor for drifting off to sleep during the sermon. The pastor, knowing well Daddy's Sunday morning routine, and maybe even enjoying the fresh milk delivered earlier that morning, replied to Daddy, "Earl, you just go ahead and enjoy your nap. If you fight to stay awake you are going to miss a good nap and a good sermon. If you get a nap at least you enjoy one of them."

It was about 1950 that Daddy and Granddaddy had a conflict of management and made the decision to close the dairy. With the dairy closed, Mom, Dad and my oldest sister moved back to Tabor City, a great joy for my mother, since she grew up in Tabor and enjoyed living in town. Country living was a trial for Mom. Dad took a job with W. F. Cox Company, a large hardware and furniture store in Tabor. He was sent to Pennsylvania to learn how to lay floor covering that was sold by the company. He returned home from training and worked for a couple of years with W. F. Cox Company. They lived in an apartment and attended Tabor City Baptist Church. Mom had grown up as a Methodist. When she married Daddy, she felt it was her place to join her husband in attending church which was of the Baptist flavor, First Baptist Loris.

It was not until my mother passed away, and I was spending much time with daddy as he battled dementia, that I learned how they came back to the farm. He shared with me that one evening while in

Tabor City, Granddaddy and Grandmother came to see him. They shared their concern about aging and the concern of being on the farm by themselves. They asked Daddy to move back to the farm and take care of them as they grew older. In return the farm, with the exception of a one-acre lot for each of the other children, would be given to him. Daddy must have asked for some time to consider it because Mom shared with me the following.

It was one evening in their apartment as they sat quietly together. Some magazines were lying on the coffee table. Mom could still see in her mind Daddy looking into a copy of The Field & Stream magazine. Daddy was just sitting there, staring at a picture in the magazine. It was a picture of a dog, sitting in a harvested field, howling at the full harvest moon. She looked at the picture and then looked at daddy. It was then that she knew the city life was over, she was headed back to "Green Acres," an old TV comedy show based on farm life.

Shortly thereafter, Mom and Dad returned to the farm. He threw himself into building a house for his growing family.

Their first year on the farm was a disaster. A severe drought that year nearly ruined the dream of farming for many. Daddy barely made it through, but with God's blessings on subsequent years, he was able to recover and establish the farm securely once more.

When I moved back to the farm, it was to help take care of my mother and father, both battling with dementia. My focus was my father who was too much for a daughter to handle. Taking care of a parent that has a dominant spirit and a strong, independent and determined mindset would be difficult enough for a son of like manner, but too much for a daughter. I therefore asked Daddy for permission to move back and be for him and Mom what he had been for Grandmother and Grandfather. He graciously accepted my offer and prepared a deed for two acres on which to build my log home.

As mentioned in my book about my journey through leukemia, "Tears of Gethsemane," I was surprised to experience my inner connection with this family farm. It was living here that renewed my heritage, of which this farm was central. However, our heritage is much more than money, land, buildings or businesses. Our heritage is part of our identity. It is the specific stream in which our lives are to be lived. It is the past which shines its guiding light upon our present and future. I therefore conclude this book and chapter with several streams of heritage that I pray will influence you to live with honor and respect within your community and extended family.

A Heritage of Caring

Earl Spivey with his father Victor
Spivey.

One of the heritage streams within our family is that of caring for family. John Edward Prince died in 1916. His wife, Mary, was only 52. She still had two children at home with her, one being my grandmother, Retha. The 1920 census lists her as living in Loris and being the head of her household. She continued to run the boarding house, as well as care for her daughters until Retha married Victor Spivey in 1919. Her daughter, Retha, and husband, Victor, moved to the Prince farm about 1930. County records indicate that in 1935, Mary Price Prince moved from the Boarding House in Loris to the home of her daughter Retha. She was 71 years of age and would remain there until her death in 1944. Her obituary states that she died in the home of her daughter Retha Prince Spivey.

As just shared, my father accepted the responsibility of being the caregiver for his mother and father. Daddy built his house only about 50 yards from Grandmother and Granddaddy. As my grandfather worsened with dementia, Daddy would check on him and Grandmother several times a day and see that all was as need be. After Granddaddy's death, Grandmother's health remained good for several years and then began to crumble. From doctor visits, to getting medicine, to buying groceries, and other necessities as well, Dad and Mom stayed true to Dad's promise. My uncles were all supportive and took much care of their mother. Some were limited by living elsewhere and could only return occasionally. Uncle Richard retired and moved back home from Chicago, in part, to help care for his mother as well. The oldest lived at the beach, about twenty miles away, and kept a careful watch over his mother as well. I have heard the wives of several of Grandmother's children comment on how devoted each of her sons were to her. During her final days a constant vigil was kept by my father and my mother as Grandmother became weaker and unable to care for herself. It was my mother that came to check on my grandmother one morning to find her complaining of an inability to breath. Since Grandmother had a history of heart trouble, my sister called for the ambulance, while my mother held Grandmother in her arms. Before the ambulance arrived, Grandmother breathed her last breath while being held in my mother's arms.

Many years later, my sisters and I were holding a family meeting, following a family meal together with Mom and Dad. We ate at my sister's house, as Mom and Dad were way beyond being able to help with the meal, and we didn't want to create so much activity in their house. Dad was still able to drive, so when they left, soon after eating, we sat looking at each other knowing the transition had arrived. We wept together, prayed together, and discussed what needed to be done.

After that meeting, I spent much time in prayer. I was a pastor. I have a calling and responsibility to shepherd Christ's flock. What part could I have in caring for the immense needs of my aging parents? My times of prayer kept taking me to two of Jesus' teachings. The first was Jesus' chastisement of the religious leaders for not providing their parents what they needed. Their religious activity was no excuse for denying their parents of their needs.

Another, was Jesus' words to John, when hanging upon the cross. He told John to take Mary as his own mother, and see that her needs were met. We are told that John did as Jesus told him, and took care of Mary until her death.

Paul punctuated it with his chastisement of the early Christian community. It seems that many were so focused on life and their plans, that mothers and fathers were being left destitute, or at the mercy of others to have their basic needs met. Paul scolded them by saying that a Christian that did not take care of their own family members were living worse than a non-Christian.

My heart was convinced. I would have to move back to the farm, and do for my mother and father what they did for my grandmother and my grandfather, as they had done for Grandmother's Mother. My focus was with my father, in particular. My sisters watched over mom with great devotion, love, and care. I kept the house up, saw that both were up in the morning, comfortable during the day, and tucked in lovingly each evening.

When I met with my church's deacons and Personnel Committee, I told them the situation, and my conviction that I must move close by to care for my parents. I offered my resignation, which they quickly refused, and asked for some time to consider the matter. They soon returned and shared with me that they were in agreement for me to move the fifteen miles away, and continue pastoring, while helping with my parents. We all wept and sought God's blessing and help in our new path together.

More than achievements, honors, and accomplishments is the family connection that binds us together. Your heritage is to care for family. Continue it honorably!

A Heritage of Placement

We naturally have desires and dreams of where we want to go in life. Yet, life is often much different than our dreams. I don't know much about my great grandparents, but I do know some about their choice to live where you are placed, and fulfill the purpose for which you are placed there.

It is obvious that John Edward Prince was born with great obstacles to overcome. Being limited in his ability to walk and use his left hand was not his choice. Being unable to play and participate in the physical acts of his siblings and others was a bitter bite to have to chew. I do know that he committed himself to getting an education and that by the age of nineteen he was a school teacher. I don't know if that was really a dream of his, or if he was filling a need he was asked to fill.

Somehow, he came to the Loris area. While here, we know he was a successful business owner of several businesses in Loris. I am told that by his early death, at sixty-six, he had become wealthy enough to provide a farm for each of his nine children. I personally know that several were given a farm, one on which I now live.

His daughter, Retha, found herself missing a dream too. One day as Grandmother and I were talking, she shared with me that she wanted to be a nurse. She was planning to go to school to be a nurse, when love struck, and she and my grandfather married. She was only sixteen. With a child soon on the way, her focus was turned to mothering, and being a housewife. It wasn't many years before her mother came to live with her. Though not trained as a nurse, she was now her mother's nurse until her mother's passing. She then continued to raise seven sons, and teach them much about the importance of hard work and pressing forward, even through life's disappointment. As she strove to see that her family was comfortably clothed and fed, she lived the role of mother to them.

It was not until I was an adult that I learned that Daddy never dreamed of living on the farm. He loved his cows, dogs, and the outdoors; but his dream was much different. One day while talking, he shared with me that he really wanted to be a lawyer. I have a couple of books he ordered, hoping to study toward getting a law degree, while still working on the farm. It was never to be. His placement was the farm, and more importantly, the caring for his mother and father.

There were many joys in his farming experience. But, the truth is, that he set aside his dream for a place that was more needed. Both the caring for parents, and the providing for a family, which had many demands.

As you may have already picked up, my mother dreamed, but it wasn't about being on a farm. She loved music and was recognized as having a promising voice. Whether in school, or church, my mother would always be found among the music groups. She loved to sing, and was asked to sing at many functions. My sister told me that mom had an opportunity to pursue a singing career in New York City waiting for her, when she graduated Tabor City High School. She chose to marry my father and live

the life of a wife and mother instead. Music was always a centerpiece in mom's life. She wanted each of her children to play the piano and participate in choir. She sacrificed more than I know, for us to take lessons and excel in music. It was with great joy, that she saw her youngest devote her life to the study and participation of music in worship and education. I, on the other hand, was the straw that broke the camel's back.

I had taken one year of piano. I enjoyed it, for the most part, and wanted to learn. The problem was practice and the annual recital. There were just too many fun things to do, and get into outside, to sit picking away at the keys on the piano. Practice had to wait till the fun stuff was done. The recital was a mental struggle for me. First, I didn't want to play in front of all the parents, and second, I couldn't understand why spending so much time on one piece of music was more important than continued lessons. So, being the independent, dominant, and even defiant personality I am, I sat at the piano banging and plucking rebelliously, day after day. Then the day came for the final straw to fall. Mom sent me to the piano while she swept the floor. Bang, bang, pluck, pluck, sigh and then -WOW, what was that? The straw fell, and my mom's frustration could be held back no longer. I felt something hit the back of my head, and turning around, saw my mother holding half a broomstick in her hand. The other half was on the floor. With tears in her eyes, and a broken heart for losing her control, she turned and walked away. I didn't play in the recital that year. The music teacher made it clear, that if anyone would not play in the recital, they would not be able to take lessons from her. I never took another lesson until my first year in college. That did not continue either. I have always regretted not being able to play the piano, but never at the price of a recital.

I never wanted to become a preacher. As I already said, I thought I would be in the music ministry. When I failed music theory, I wept, because I had no idea of what direction to take. As I sought

God's guidance, I just felt at peace switching to a major in Bible, and a minor in Christian education. My actual dream for life was to either become a missionary to a far-away people group needing spiritual guidance, or being a college professor. Even after thirty plus years of pastoring, I feel the sorrow of never having been either. Is that to say my life has been a failure? Heaven's no! My following the path God unfolded before me has been filled with great joy and reward. I wouldn't go back and change it. But I must admit it wasn't my chosen and desired path.

When my wife, Lauretta, and I married, forty-one years ago, I had many dreams. Most of them came from the emptiness and loneliness within me. Unrealistic, self-focused, and certainly, not aimed at a healthy relationship, my dreams were soon dashed upon the rock of reality. My wife and I, despite my being a minister, of which we are human too, after all, have struggled and forced our way to maintain our marriage of forty-one years. We struggled through the reality of not being able to have children. She grieved over the dreams she had, that I was not fulfilling. We clung to our faith and held to the Bible's instructions. Is our marriage a failure? NO! We look back over the years and thank God for the great times shared together. We rejoice that our relationship has grown to a respect, and appreciation of one another, rather than an emotional fulfilling of a lesser need. We celebrate the ways we have served God together, and live grateful for the companionship and support we have given each other through life. Is it the marriage we dreamed? No. But it is where we were placed. And through it we have been bettered and enriched, personally and spiritually.

I did not plan to become a father at forty-five. The door swung open, and again, at forty-six; so we walked through it without hesitation. Though many unexpected events have taken place, and unforeseen pathways have been taken, I thank God for the journey and would not change it even if I could. Your heritage is to recognize your place and live it to your fullest! Make the most of life wherever you are placed, it's your heritage.

The Heritage of Community

When John Edward Prince came to Loris there wasn't a Loris. When the small handful of merchants and people living by a new railroad came together, John Edward Prince was among them. They wanted to see a safe, prospering, and

*stable community established, where they could
live and raise their families. So, in mutual
agreement, they petitioned the state of South
Carolina to recognize the new community of Loris
as a town, and henceforth placed on the map of
South Carolina. In the 1900's, there was more to
being a successful business person than
prosperity. A business had to pay for itself, and
more for those working in it for sure. However,
businesses rose with a sense of purpose to the
community. The hotels, hardware and furniture
store, bank, blacksmith shop, barber shop, drug
store, dry goods, warehouses and more grew out of
needs within the community. The town leaders
united in an effort to build a high school, which
was much needed in Loris. It seems to me that
business for the purpose of serving our
community, has given way to a thirst to make a
profit, and enjoy the good life.*

*When my grandfather, Victor, returned home, he
saw a need glaring before him. The boys of Loris
needed guidance in becoming men, who would
build a healthy and prospering community. His
solution was an organization called Boy Scouts of
America. He became the scout master, and began
investing much time and energy in being a
positive influence to the young boys of Loris. I
have some of the camping equipment my
grandfather used. I have other items that remind
me of his work of trying to make Loris a better
place through the avenue of Boy Scouts.*

He was instrumental in the Lion's Club in Loris. He encouraged the athletic program at the High School. When Santee Cooper Electric Company wanted to run a powerline into Loris, they needed permission from the many land owners to run it across their property. I'm sure that most all were in agreement to give them permission for the betterment of the Loris community. My grandfather saw an opportunity to do something for the school athletic program as well. When the representative from Santee Cooper came to talk with him, he was ready. They asked, "Mr. Spivey we are here to ask permission to run a powerline across your property into the town of Loris."

"Ok," Granddaddy said, "with one condition."

The representative braced himself for the condition.

"If you will provide the poles and lights to light the school football field, I will give you my permission."

I don't think it was much of a consideration on Santee Cooper's part, as they saw it as a good publicity act for the community. They kept their agreement and now the practice and games were able to be held at night.

Granddaddy chose to involve himself in ways to better his community and those living around him. Once when my youngest uncle and I were able to visit my grandfather's niece, she shared some about Granddaddy and Grandmother's community spirit.

She told of how when her father drank and left the family without food and necessities: "Uncle Victor and Aunt Retha would time and again show up on our doorstep with a box of food and whatever other supplies were needed." It wasn't just them but many others. Community is our extended family, and they need our care too.

We may have lived outside the Loris City limits, but we still saw ourselves as part of the Loris community. My father, and several others, grew concerned as our community moved from horse and buggy to automobiles. As the vehicles became more powerful, and faster, crashes were sure to occur. They gathered together and agreed to form The Loris Volunteer Rescue Squad. They had no government or community financial support. They saw a need, and committed to fill it, even if they had to subsidize it themselves. At first, the funeral home used the hearse to transport injured persons to the hospital, another story of community effort. Funny stories were told of injured persons seeing the funeral home hearse coming, only to run in fear of being taken to the funeral home, instead of the hospital. They eventually purchased a white van that could be used. I would sometimes go into the bathroom and see Daddy's bloody clothing soaking in the tub. He had gone to a wreck, and in helping the injured, become wet in their blood.

They were often called to recover the body of a drowning victim. I recall going with Daddy on a couple of just such occasions. One was at a pond, where several boys, hot from working in tobacco, jumped into the pond to cool off. One jumped in but never came out. The Rescue Squad was called, and a handful of men converged on the farm. They brought a boat and a heavy wire square with ropes for pulling, and fish hooks attached to snare the body. As the hooks caught in the skin of the young boy, they pulled the lifeless body to shore, with many fighting back tears in their eyes. Daddy wanted me to see the body so I would not follow in the young boy's steps. I was too afraid and stayed in the car.

Another came on an afternoon at Red Bluff. Red Bluff was a favorite swimming spot on the Waccamaw River about fifteen miles east of Loris. Again, I jumped in, as daddy rushed to help. When we arrived, the boat was already in the river dragging, as they called it, for the body submerged somewhere below. They did not snag the body with the dragging, so another method was tried. Thinking the body may be at the base of one of the pilings for the bridge, they used a long pole with a couple of hooks attached to the end. I stood on the bank watching, when the men in the boat grew quiet, and one said, "Men, I think we found him." They slowly pulled the body to the surface and over to the bank. The lesson was sinking in. It *wasn't to be fearful and scared of water. It was to use caution and good sense knowing water is as deadly as guns. Used correctly, it is fun and an important tool. But take it too lightly, and you will not be given a second chance.*

One more, and I will move on. The one that shook up my father most occurred late one evening. The phone rang, and they were called out to find a missing boy, that had left to go fishing, and had not returned home. My mother told me what took place. They gathered all the information they could, and fanned out looking for him. Fearing he could have drowned or become lost in the woods, they felt it urgent to locate him. Before long, the familiar word, "Over here, over here," rang through the night air. They all converged around a lifeless body with a fishing pole and can of worms. Upon closer examination it was discovered that the boy had dug some worms for bait before going to the fishing hole. Being young, and not knowing better, he had dug into the nest of a rattlesnake. What he thought were worms, were instead baby snakes biting and unloading their full load of vinum. That was a nightmare enough, but the boy had many features like me. Mom said Daddy came home with tears in his eyes and went straight to my bed. He looked, gently touched, and wept some more.

Today, few recall, or even know about, the Cuban Missile Crisis. In 1962, Russia, in agreement with Cuba, brought in nuclear missiles only ninety miles from Florida. A long and tense month of talk, threats, and negotiations was spent between the USA and Russia. It was resolved peacefully, but now, America had changed. I was only six years old and oblivious to world affairs. I only remember Daddy bringing home boxes of yellow instruments labeled, "Civil Defense." The rescue squad was now thrust into the nuclear age. People were trained on how to detect nuclear radiation and what to do if detecting it. Thankfully, we never had to use any of them.

My story is less noble. When my wife and I moved to Indiana, I joined others from various churches in taking part in a clothing and food pantry. From week to week, I would help sift through, organize, and assist those seeking clothing or food. Another involvement in helping others came through the church family where I pastored. I had preached and promoted our humanitarian compassion in the name of Jesus Christ. I do not remember where the idea first originated, but it arose, and many eagerly came to help. We discovered that Meals on Wheels, which provided one meal a day, to the many unable to prepare a balanced meal, closed on holidays. That meant, each Thanksgiving, the many depending upon Meals on Wheels, would spend their day eating whatever they had left, or could find. The idea was proposed to give our Thanksgiving Day, in an act of love, from Christ, to our community. We spread the word, and began preparing for a meal of love.

The calls soon came in, and on our first Thanksgiving, we served over 300 meals. I helped make deliveries, while the others made plates of Turkey, dressing, green beans, bread, and more, as plates were being packed for another run. At 5:00 that afternoon I was still delivering. From that first day it grew to over 1000 meals being provided by our church, and others, that joined with us. This was being done by a small church, with barely thirty on a good Sunday.

The church I served, when I returned to South Carolina was in a very rural area. With the loss of farm laborers, migrants from Mexico, and Central America came to fill the empty places. I participated in a ministry to provide worship and Biblical instruction to the adults. We also saw that many children were being left unattended by adults, or kept in a vehicle at the edge of the field, while their parents worked. My fourth-grade teacher was a member of the church, and we discussed what we could do. We decided to start a weekly club, "Club de Jesus," as a way to share the Bible with the children, and give them a fun and enjoyable time away.

On one particular day, I was using my car to gather up the children. I had gotten to know many of the adult workers, and they had given me permission to go to their houses and get their children, and bring them back after the meeting. On this day, one little boy was very inquisitive, and God used it for a lesson. As we talked, he caught on to me saying something about growing up on a farm.

"Does your daddy own his land?"

"Yes," I replied

"Does he have cows?" he asked.

"Yes, he has twenty or thirty I guess."

"Then you are rich," he said.

I first started to deny being rich but stopped to think. All I could say was, "I guess you are right, I am rich." I whispered a prayer, "Father, forgive me, for making being poor convenient. Help me realize how wealthy I am, and my responsibility to use it in serving You."

The most recent ministry involvement is one God started through me several years ago. We call it, "Bethesda for Single Mothers." The focus is to provide a safe place for single mothers and their child, or children, to stay so they can reestablish their lives. As I saw young mothers drowning in helplessness, God spoke to my heart about providing a place, where they could discover God's love, and a helping hand to build a joyful and secure family. It would require of them much time and great determination. But as we see girls taking advantage of such an opportunity, it is more than rewarding to witness the hopeless refreshed in renewed hope. To see those, who have been broken and crushed by life, and bad choices, experiencing a turnaround, that gives them a real hope of one day, living financially stable, and with the peace and hope, that only Jesus Christ can give, is greatly rewarding.

There are many other stories I could tell of being community minded. Remember this: "Life is about your community, not you!" If you want the world to be a better world, start by helping your community become a better community. After all, its part of your heritage.

A Heritage of Faith

John Edwards Prince family Bible.
c1880

"Therefore, since we are surrounded by such a great cloud of witnesses...let us run with perseverance the race marked out for us." Hebrews 12:1 (NIV)

John Edward's daughter, Retha, received from her father an enduring and sincere faith. Even though, she was only thirteen when he died, she had seen the patterns and evidences of a faith that outwardly affected his living. I am told that, though, she lived one mile south of Loris, she would dress her children and walk with them one mile down the railroad tracks to Main Street in Loris, and then walk the five blocks west to Loris First Baptist Church. My grandmother never had a license to drive a car. I am sure there were many times that a horse and buggy were used as well, but it is evident, that her faith was sincere enough to compel her to worship with her church family, even when difficult and inconvenient to do so.

Several of her sons gave evidence of inheriting that faith. My father was one of them. While still living at home and starting the dairy, around nineteen years old, he began teaching a Sunday School class. He had attended church with his mother, and earlier made a public announcement to declare his faith in Jesus Christ as God's Son, and the source of his forgiveness, and promise of eternal life. He took Jesus and the Bible seriously. Even at that early age, he was committed to studying the Bible and teaching others what the Bible instructs us.

My mother was much the same. She grew up just a block from St. Paul United Methodist Church in Tabor City. She and her father walked to church Sunday after Sunday. I recall visiting with them on Sunday afternoons and reading the bulletin my Grandfather Elliott brought home from church that morning. He strove to pass down his faith to his children, and my mother received it with depth and sincerity.

When she and my father met, their commitment to live under God's instruction and authority was essential, before considering a serious interest in one another. How did a young man from Loris and a High School girl from Tabor City meet?

My Grandmother Elliott, Mom's mother, had several siblings, of course. One of those lived in Loris, and had a son that became a doctor. He had a house and clinic on 701 South in Loris. Dr. Rogers was his name. His mother stayed with him, and mom would frequently ride the train, for the short seven-mile trip, over to stay with her aunt, for a day or two. My father's first cousin happened to be my mother's close friend. Mary Cooper told my mother about my father, and introduced them to each other. Their interest in each other grew until mom and dad agreed to unite into a life-long relationship together.

As my Grandmother Elliott was most disturbed about her daughter having a serious relationship with some "farmer," Mom kept their plans secret. When the agreed upon day arrived, Dad drove to Tabor City and, as they routinely did, drove off together. However, this day they came to Loris, stopped to see the preacher, and made their life-long vows of love and devotion to God and one another, just prior to singing in the Easter cantata. They sent word to my grandmother who was greatly displeased.

Mom and Dad first stayed with Grandmother and Granddaddy Spivey. They attended Loris First Baptist, as that was Dad's church home. After moving back to Loris in 1954 and Mom's being baptized into the Baptist Church, both parents became involved in church life. After working in the nursery for many years, Mom's devotion to Christ and depth of sincerity shown through and she, too, was asked to teach a Sunday School Class. She did, until she was mentally unable to do so, due to dementia.

When Mom and Dad resigned from teaching due to their poor health, they were both honored by the church. Dad had been teaching for 60+ consecutive years. Mom had taught for 50+ consecutive years. I can remember, on numerous occasions, seeing Mom and Dad sitting with their Sunday School lesson book laid open, and the Bible open beside it, as they worked to prepare their lesson for the class the coming Sunday. Some *of my treasured items are a stack of note pads, my mother used to outline her lesson for her Sunday School class. I have read through them, letting my mother's teachings speak to me as well.*

Already mentioned is my mother's love for music. She was always in the choir and often the soloist. Yet, her devotion was evident in other ways as well.

One of mom's loves was for children. She seemed, even though teaching an adult women's Sunday School class, to always be involved in the children's area of the church's work. She taught in the children's department, youth department and other areas of the church's work. Maybe, that had something to do with having five children, taking a span of about thirty years, to raise them to adulthood. But, it was more than that. From Vacation Bible School to Child Evangelism Fellowship, and even, Mom's day to day work with the children at school, she was busy loving, and teaching children about the faith so foundational to her living each day.

When I went back to college, I learned of some children in a poor section near the school. I felt burdened to gather them together for a time of Bible teaching and Christian fun. I went straight to mom. She brought out the flannelgraph stories and figures from years earlier. She pulled out the visual aids for songs as well. She gave them to me with her blessings, and in great joy that a heritage was being passed down.

Attending church on Sunday was just the norm for my family. I remember being so set in the pattern of getting ready for church, that it was just the routine thing we did. I had awoken one morning and started getting ready for the day. I put on my Sunday clothes and shoes, and then ran to enjoy some breakfast. When I arrived at the table, my sisters were giggling. They, then, told me it was only Saturday morning. I had thought it was Sunday, and knew that if it was Sunday, we were going to church.

Mom and Dad served in many areas of the church's work. They were also devoted to Gideons International and other Christian community ministries. It was all part of being participants in a people worshiping, and serving God, in the way they believed it should be done. From both sides of my gene pool, faith was demonstrated and lived out before me. My embracing of this faith came not by coercion or pressure, but by the melting of my heart instead.

Mom and Dad prayed for each of their children before we were conceived, while she was pregnant, and every day, once we were born. On more than one occasion I would run to Mom and Dad's bedroom, after being put in bed to find them on their knees praying for their children. God was not an escape from eternal punishment to them. He was their comfort, hope, peace and Helper for the journey of life.

Once God melted my heart, I began to discover this faith that I had observed as a child. It had been passed down, and was now, my personal faith too. My experiences in college and seminary deepened my understandings and insights into this faith, built upon the teachings of Jesus Christ. A faith modeled and intentionally shared, with the prayer that their children would one day inherit their faith, and join their parents in a personal devotion to Jesus Christ.

It was perhaps Mom and Dad's greatest joy to see all five of their children embracing the faith they had embraced from their parents as well. Now a new generation was living with their own convictions, and confidence in the faith that has been passed down since Jesus taught His disciples. To see my sisters and I making Jesus Christ the dominant influence, and the Bible being our guide brought great joy to my parents. They had lived their lives praying for us, their children, to carry the torch they had held. When they saw their prayers and hard labors fulfilled, they rejoiced, and felt that one of life's most important works was accomplished successfully, and with great personal rewards.

Each of us, their children, have carried our torch of faith with the intent that our children and others around us would join us by carrying their torch of faith, too. After all, that is what Christ demonstrated, and taught His followers, to teach those joining them on this journey of faith. Faith in God as the Supreme Ruler, and Jesus Christ as His Son bringing to this world light and eternal hope, is not just discovered. It is a revelation given us by God, Himself. It is passed down from one person to another. It is learned from and encouraged, by others around us. The New Testament is clear that believers in Christ, and followers of Christ, form a community and are not isolated individuals.

I, therefore, challenge you who are reading this book, my children, and whoever else is allowing me to guide you in thinking about your heritage; to reflect upon your spiritual heritage. You, my children, have watched my living from your earliest days. My being a pastor was a sincere effort to do what I believed God had chosen for me to do. My desire was to be faithful and obedient to the one who released me from my wrongs, freed me to live by the enlightenment Jesus Himself taught, and to anticipate a coming world, where God rules uncontested by any opposition, and gathers His worshipers in a world free from any wrong, hurt or evil ways. It is my sincere desire to ignite the torch of faith you have been given with the fire of my torch of faith. I do not give you a way of life. I give you a faith that becomes your light and guide for living.

You have a rich, and enduring spiritual heritage. Examine it, explore it, give sincere consideration to the source, historical record and evidences revealed in the lives of your ancestors. Then in the

*words of Joshua, to the Jews now in firm control
of the Promised Land, "...then choose for
yourselves this day whom you will serve, whether
the gods your forefathers served beyond the River,
or the gods of the Amorites, in whose land you are
living. But as for me and my household, we will
serve the LORD." Joshua 24:15 (NIV)*

*This is one choice each person must make for
themself. I encourage you, let your heritage lead
you in making your choice.*

From the John Edwards Prince family
Bible

Rev. Earl J. Spivey Jr. grew up on a small farm in Northeastern South Carolina. He attended Central Wesleyan College, now Southern Wesleyan University, earning a BA degree in Bible and Christian education. He attended Southeastern Baptist Theological Seminary, receiving a master's of divinity and religious education degree. Following seminary, he pastored in Indiana before returning to South Carolina. He pastored Southern Baptist Convention churches for twenty-eight years. Most were in South Carolina. He has been involved with Methodist, Presbyterian, and Episcopalian pastors and churches in ecumenical activities. He has a wife of forty-two years and two children. Being a disciple of Christ and student of the Bible has been a foundation for his life.

He is presently the executive director of Bethesda for Single Mothers. Its focus is to be a Christian community giving single mothers a place to live while completing their education and keeping their children. The goal is to enable mothers to return to society financially secure and spiritually solid. He has also completed a discipleship manual, Parental Disciple Makers, that will lead the participants to make the necessary commitments to follow and live in submission to Christ with sincerity. He is actively leading men in this discipleship journey. Rev. Spivey has also written "Tears of Gethsemane,

A Pastor's Journey through Leukemia." In it he shares his experiences through AML and spiritual insights in dealing with life threatening illnesses. He is available for speaking engagements and other special events. Contact the author at meadowlawnministries@gmail.com. Learn more at meadowlawministries.com.